Contents

Acknowledgements

When writing the acknowledgements for the first edition, I expressed my debt to the many people I have learned from in my career as a trainer. Many I have never met, and they in turn are unlikely to have ever heard of me. As best I can, I acknowledge their contribution to my development and to this book in the bibliography. While I have not referenced the book, I have tried to provide original sources in the text and the bibliography is, I think, extensive and well worth using for guidance on further reading. There are also those I have worked with in retail, in local government and in higher education. Colleagues are a much underrated and underutilized source of development. I have been fortunate to work with many who have willingly and effectively furthered my learning. There are those, too, whom I have tried to educate and train. If they have gained as much from me as I have from them, the efforts of us all will have been worthwhile.

Three other people who deserve my public thanks are Laura – for bearing the burden of reading my handwriting to turn the book into a legible, typed manuscript – and, most importantly, my wife Pat and son Paul for their patience and support in excusing me from my family activities. In addition, I wish to thank Sheila for applying her excellent typing skills in producing the revisions for this second edition, and the staff at Kogan Page, especially Dolores Black, for their help and support in getting my work published. This book, however, represents a personal view and as such neither you nor I can blame anyone but me for its mistakes and weaknesses.

Foreword

The word 'change' now has a familiar ring in organizations of all kinds. It is a word which is likely to evoke anxiety and sometimes fear for those who believe in the maxim that 'nothing good comes out of change'. For others it is a signal for challenge and exciting times ahead and for some it is perceived as an alarm bell to begin a fight for personal or departmental survival. There is an element of truth in all of these reactions but change should not be regarded as all 'doom and gloom'. Old dogs can be taught new tricks and people of all age groups, personality types, skill and employment backgrounds are often surprised by their adaptability and contribution to change.

As organizations compete to become more effective by making better use of their resources the human resource comes under close scrutiny in terms of its skill and experience and how far they match the needs for meeting future organizational goals. In those organizations that are used to change and where change is seen as evolution rather than revolution, fear and anxiety are not so likely to exist. Such organizations have learned how to handle change; they have learned how to involve everyone, they have learned how to communicate and they have learned how to initiate and introduce change. They have become learning organizations.

Such learning does not come about by accident. It needs to be fostered by effective management of change. The responsibility for this does not immediately register in the mind as belonging to any particular deparment or function but on consideration it can be appreciated that it is a training and development role. In making this claim it is not a case of trainers engaging in empire-building but putting to wider use the skills and techniques in which they are well practised.

First, the methodologies and techniques of investigation and analysis used by trainers are highly relevant to the conduct of studies in the wider organizational context and to the development of the organization as a whole. Second, any change in the way in which an organization operates is likely to involve changes in the jobs that people perform and the way in which they perform them. This makes training and development an integral part of the process and gives trainers more varied roles to play.

In order to take on such roles, the professional function of the trainer needs to change. The training department cannot stand still while change is taking place all around it. It is not new for trainers to describe their roles as 'agents for change' and while this may have seemed a little trite or pretentious in the past, it is clearly appropriate today. As the value of training departments and professional trainers gains more recognition and representation at board level and subsequently greater involvement in the implementation of corporate strategy, so the need grows for trainers to increase their knowledge and develop their skills in those areas which they may not have had the opportunity to exploit in the past.

In this book, Jim Stewart draws upon his experience as a training and development consultant who has worked with a number of large organizations. In doing so, he shows why the training and development function should be closely involved with organizational development and how trainers can apply their skills and methodology to this vitally important area. It is clearly a practical book but one that also brings out the theoretical underpinnings which help trainers to develop their roles with confidence and to play a pro-active role in the implementation and management of change.

Roger Buckley
Manager (Trainer Training)
National Westminster Bank plc
September 1991

1. About this book

INTRODUCTION

At the time of writing the first edition of this book, I was able to identify a number of significant changes occurring across the world. These included the reunification of Germany and democratization of the former communist bloc countries in central and Eastern Europe. These examples illustrate the unpredictability of change, since neither would have been forecast perhaps even five years before they happened.

I also mentioned another set of examples, including the end of the 'cold war' and the emergence of capitalist ideology as the leading force in economics and world politics. The distinction between the two sets of examples lay in the perceived difference between change as an 'event' and change as a 'process'. The first examples suggest a more-or-less permanent shift from one set of conditions to another set of conditions. In other words, the change *has happened*. Germany is now unified and many former communist countries now have democratic political systems. The second examples suggest that change happens over time since capitalism is becoming increasingly predominant. In other words, the change *is happening*.

The dominance or otherwise of capitalism is of course subject to much academic debate. There are those who argue what is termed a convergence thesis, which predicts increasing homogeneity in economic and political systems across the world. Others argue that variation in historical and cultural traditions will ensure that such homogeneity will not be achieved.

Whichever analysis and prediction holds most validity is of minor interest to this work. What is of most interest and concern is that whether change is seen as an event or as a process, anticipating the implications and predicting the consequences is an almost impossible task. Certainly this is true at the level of global politics and economics. I would argue that there are only two certainties. First, that the future is uncertain. Second, that any particular or specific change will generate other changes. Thus, we can conclude that change is both continuous and uncertain.

The examples quoted are drawn from the world of politics. I do not mean to imply that other features are either not changing or that they are of no significance. Examples of significant change abound from the worlds of science and technology, and these have significant economic and social consequences. Two examples are advances in biogenetics and the widespread availability of access to the information superhighway. The former has tremendous potential in the field of medical treatment, but also highlights and produces serious social issues. Similarly, the latter promises great potential in terms of access to information and raises important questions about the nature and function of social interaction.

We can then argue a condition of widespread global change as the backdrop to this book. Continuous, uncertain, unpredictable and sudden change is a condition of living in the latter part of the twentieth century which will become even more the case in the twenty-first. Learning to cope with and manage that condition is, in my view, the single most important challenge facing the world today. Since it is a challenge facing the world, it is a challenge facing you and me and the organizations in which we work.

THE CONTEXT

A cursory survey of the titles and content of recent books on management, and the titles and content of current management education and training programmes, would reveal 'change' and 'change management' as probably the subjects most often referred to. Such a result would suggest that the interest in managing change in organizations is growing with the rate of change itself. This is to be welcomed, however, since it indicates a recognition of the urgency of the challenge.

Global politics, biogenetics and the information superhighway are not of course of direct interest or concern to all organizations. The work of Peter Senge, discussed in a later chapter, would suggest that such subjects are, at least, of indirect concern to all organizations. It is the case that global politics is likely to be critical to only multinational corporations and medium to large organizations that seek to maintain and develop their success through export and international trade. However it is also the case that even the smallest organization has to take account of two factors. First, changes in global politics and scientific knowledge create economic and social consequences which impact on national and more local geographical markets. Coping with and managing responses to these changes will be critical for the survival of the smallest business. Second, change is being

experienced at a growing rate in all economic sectors. Many of these changes are specific to particular national or regional economies. So, the challenge of managing change has to be faced by all organizations, large or small, industrial or commercial or publicly owned, service or marketing or production oriented.

Increasing Commercialization

Increasing Competition

Customer Sovereignty

A Need for Personal/Individual Accountability and Control

Technological Advancement

Shifts in State Intervention

Political Influences

Fundamental Social Change

Demographic Change

Figure 1.1   *Changes facing organizations in the 1990s*
(Source: Stewart, 1990b)

To support this argument and illustrate the context, Figure 1.1 summarizes the results of a research project I undertook into the changing role of management development practitioners. The results of my research at the beginning of the 1990s found support in an international study conducted by the UK-based Ashridge Management Research Group, which identified similar economic and technological factors impacting on organizations. The 'triggers for change' identified by Ashridge are:

- Financial losses.
- Drop in profits.
- Increased competition.
- Loss of market share.
- Industry in recession.
- Technological development.
- Staff utilization.

Research conducted between 1993 and 1995 with senior HRM practitioners confirms this earlier picture (Stewart and Sambrook, 1995). Practitioners continue to report factors such as technology, competition, state policies and demographic features as significant environmental variables which are subject to continuous change. The critical condition then, in which organizations operate as we approach the start of a new century, is that of constant change. That is the context on which this book is based.

THE PURPOSE

The responsibility within organizations for responding to change rests with management. In this sense, as Drucker recognized (Stoner, 1989), 'management' is a collective noun that defines those people in the organization who have the word in their job title and/or are charged with making decisions to ensure current and long-term survival. A Chief Executive I once interviewed (Stewart, 1990) had as a declared aim the achievement of an organization where *all* employees at all levels take responsibility for managing themselves as a resource and as a provider of services. Watson (1994) similarly argues that managers at all levels have strategic impact in that their decisions and actions affect long term survival.

Generally senior managers have to manage change; training and development is also their responsibility. The primary purpose of this book is to demonstrate how development interventions can be used to help manage change. My intention is to explain why and how training and development activities are a critical component in coping with and responding to change. Given that purpose and the previous argument on development being a management responsibility, the book is relevant to all managers from any function. However, I do adopt the specialist focus of training and development and, being a development professional, naturally have that as my personal perspective. The content of the book is perhaps of most interest to human resource management (HRM) and human resource development (HRD) practitioners.

My purpose is to provide an overview of the relationship between managing change and the practice of training and development. That the former is critical to long-term success is now accepted. That there is a relationship between organization success and training and development is also now well recognized (Moorby, 1991; Buckley and Caple, 1994). My argument here is that without a conscious, well-planned and professionally delivered training and development component, any strategy for managing change is likely to be deficient.

A second purpose is to attempt to draw together a number of strands of thought about both managing change and training and development. The growing provision of books and development programmes has led to the terminology becoming confused. Different meanings are attached to the same concepts and phrases: a situation that creates difficulty in making informed decisions. I hope therefore to provide a framework for analysis which will make it easier to compare and contrast different, or competing, approaches and to reach effective decisions in relating strategy to purpose.

THE CONTENT AND STRUCTURE

This book concentrates on approaches to and methods of managing change which either involve or are directly related to recognized development interventions. What I mean by this is that there exists a range of methods which are commonly recognized to fall within the ambit of HRM professionals in general and training professionals in particular. Much recent research and debate among both academics and practitioners has focused on the need for those involved in HRM to adopt a more strategic and managerial role in organizations, and to relate their practice much more closely to the strategic direction and business needs of organizations (see McGoldrick and Stewart, 1996). Given that we have established that those needs include the management of change, HRM practice has to offer a real contribution to achieving organizational effectiveness in that area if it is to remain relevant. The content of the book therefore focuses on describing development methods and interventions which can be applied to support the management of change, and on examining their practical implementation.

There is ample evidence that many HRM/HRD specialists are not yet providing the kind of contribution required by organizations. The role of the Development Professional is certainly changing. Research indicates a role in transition from direct provider to that of Organization Development Consultant and agent for change. While this role is not an entirely new phenomenon, it is becoming both more common and more important. Its operation requires working understanding of research and theory from the social sciences. The approaches and methods included in this book are chosen to enable practitioners to take on this emerging role and to apply appropriate methods and techniques in their practice.

The framework I have adopted to structure the content reflects three levels of change. These are the level of the organization, the group or team, and the individual. Such a framework is now commonly applied, especially when thinking or writing about notions such as the learning organization (see Chapter 6). Chapters 3 to 6 examine theories, models and methods which are particularly relevant to change throughout, or at the level of, the organization. Chapters 7, 8 and 9 focus on change at the level of the group or team. Chapters 10 and 11 examine change at the level of the individual.

This division of the three levels should not be taken to imply that they are mutually exclusive. In fact, it is difficult in practice to separate the levels and to work in or at one level in isolation from the other two. However, I believe the division provides a useful analytical framework for thinking about the role and purpose of different approaches and methods. It is recognized though that any strategy for managing change will need to utilize methods from all three levels. A successful strategy will also need to integrate all three levels.

The chapter which follows this introduction provides some ideas on the nature of change as experienced by organizations, and draws on lessons that might be learned from the phenomenon of change as it naturally occurs in the functioning of the planet. The final chapter of the book returns to this speculative theme and introduces two models I have formulated to provide an overall concept of managing change through training and development.

THE NATURE AND USE OF THE BOOK

The content of this chapter so far betrays a particular perspective on the nature of organizations and the meaning of management. It needs to be acknowledged that my perspective is one which is subject to questioning and challenge. Many writers on organizations and management would more than query my assumption that organizations can usefully be believed to have some form of independent, or 'objective' existence, or that the interests of management can coincide with the interests of non-management (eg, Watson, 1994; Legge, 1995). The nature of reality, the 'causes' of human behaviour and the best, or most effective, ways of serving human interests are subject to much wider debate than that represented by organization and management theory. The line of academic enquiry and writing known as postmodernism challenges the assumed nature of human existence and experience in relation to any conception of objective reality (Fisher, 1996). Research in biology and into the role of genes (Dawkins, 1989) and debates surrounding the validity and application of Social Darwinism extend and renew the established divisions on the role of nature and nurture in human behaviour. The competing analyses referred to earlier on the world spread of capitalism engage debates on the potential of economic systems to serve the interests of *all* human beings. I cannot examine these arguments here. For the purpose of this book, I take it as axiomatic that organizations can *usefully* be thought of as objective entities, that human behaviour can be influenced and that collective economic interests can be served through the processes of management.

A careful and analytical reader will also probably find it possible to identify inconsistencies and perhaps even contradictions in the content. This is because the book is essentially a personal statement of my own views on the subjects included. It is also because theories, in common with all other aspects of life, are like that; they can be shown to contradict each other at an intellectual level while at the same time have value in practice. (For those who are interested that is, almost, a postmodern argument!) One example of this is the existence of competing theories of learning which have obvious inherent inconsistencies when compared with each other, but which also are all very practical and useful in designing learning opportunities.

My concern then is not with establishing truth or validity. Rather, it is with writing a book of practical value which contains concepts and ideas which can be usefully applied. For this reason, I am not out to impress with intellectual argument. What I describe has been of value to me in my own practice and my hope and intention is that this will be the case for others. Management, whether science or art, is above all else pragmatic and I think what does, or might, work is what matters most.

Following from this approach the book is both academic and non-academic. It is academic in the sense that I provide expositions of relevant theories which I believe need to be understood. It is non-academic in the sense that I do this by explaining them in simple terms that make sense to me. In doing so I may do their originators some injustice but at least they can take comfort from their application and use. The book also contains some theorizing and models of my own. In all cases I try to support application with examples and/or case studies.

I have attempted to provide a cohesive and integrated overview of many different approaches and methods which draws on a wide range of sources. However, this does not mean that the book has to be read straight through from start to finish. It is possible to gain something useful from individual chapters. For instance, some chapters concentrate on explaining underlying theories in preparation for examining methods. Those less interested in theory can go straight to application chapters. Similarly, if current work focuses on the total organization or team development then those chapters can be read first. I hope the book will provide a useful continuing reference work that can be dipped into as and when required.

SOME INITIAL DEFINITIONS

A final consideration to close this introduction is to establish some working definitions. There are four critical terms that require establishment of a common understanding. The first of these, *change*, is defined in a later chapter. It is sufficient to say here that change simply means that something is different. That may seem a trite statement, but it is important and accurate. Managing change is managing different circumstances. The other terms requiring definition are discussed below.

Management

Management, or managing, is essentially a process of agreeing and achieving organization objectives. This definition implies the potential of serving collective interests and suggests that the nature of managing is more concerned with *enabling* than with control. In the context of change, managing means anticipating, responding and initiating to ensure change and change processes happen in a way that supports the agreement and achievement of objectives. It means that those changes which can be most easily decided and influenced, ie, those within the organization, are appropriate to meet the demands of those changes most difficult to influence and manage, ie, those outside the organization. Managers are responsible for ensuring that they and the organization have the flexibility to utilize change for positive or beneficial results. This point is illustrated in Figure 1.2.

Work organizations

I use the term 'work organization' and the word 'organization' synonymously throughout the book. Both refer to collections of individuals organized into a recognizable social system for the purpose of producing and providing some goods or services. In common with Watson (1994), I view the social system as a set of ongoing human relationships. Normally, two key features of the relationships which characterize an organization are the application of the concepts of employer and employee and the existence of a hierarchical structure to govern the distribution of power. My definition is intended to include all such social systems irrespective of which sector of the economy they operate within. It can also be applied to sub-systems such as divisions, business units, profit centres or functional departments. Such sub-systems can for the purposes of this book be regarded as separate and independent organizations.

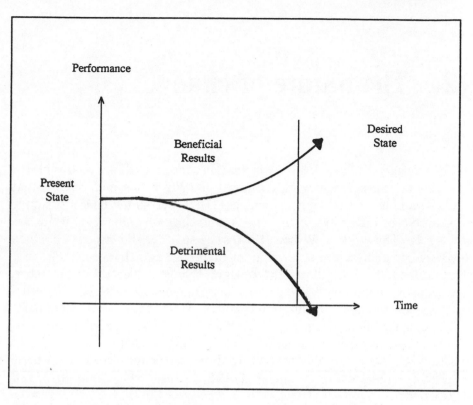

Figure 1.2   *The result of managed versus unmanaged change*

Training and development

Training and development refers to the organization function which has the aim of ensuring that the contribution of individuals and groups to the agreement and achievement of organization objectives is maximized through the development of appropriate knowledge, skills and attitudes. Its contribution to organization performance and effectiveness is primarily through the development of people as individuals, as work groups and as members of the wider organization. The distinction between training and development and HRD, and the relationship between both or either, and HRM, is not unproblematic (McGoldrick and Stewart, 1996). However, I use terms such as HRM and HRD practitioners and trainers synonymously throughout the book. In my view, all such practitioners need to be able to perform this function, to engage in the process of HRD and to provide a development contribution.

2. The nature of change

The management of change is of increasing concern to those responsible for the continued success of work organizations. Why is this; and what is it that organizations are seeking to manage? These questions have no simple answers – or rather lots of answers with no clear way of judging which are 'correct'. The work of Wilson (1992) suggests three dimensions on which competing analyses and prescriptions of change and change management can differ. These are the extent to which change is planned or emergent, whether it is voluntary on the part of management or determined by external forces, and whether organization change is evolutionary or revolutionary. This chapter will not claim to provide 'right answers' or a definitive analysis. It will instead explore the nature and meaning of change as a means of setting a context for what follows. In doing so, possible answers to these difficult questions may emerge based on my own perspective and experience.

One feature of the growing interest in change management that I find particularly interesting is the implication that change is somehow a new phenomenon that presents an unprecedented challenge. While this is patently not the case, it does seem hard on occasions to demonstrate to managers that they have successfully managed change in the past, and are currently doing so. It is in the nature of human social systems, including societies and work organizations, that they change over time. Therefore, managers of work organizations must by definition be attempting to manage change, albeit well or badly. This argument can be further illuminated by taking the example of the changing nature of societies. Some historical periods appear to have enough internal consistency around a significant feature of social organization to justify an easily recognizable label to identify and differentiate them from other periods. Thus, we can quote the 'Stone Age', 'Bronze Age' and 'Iron Age'. Or, more recently, the 'Industrial' or 'Machine Age' which preceded the current 'Information Age'. These labels demonstrate that societies do change over time, but even the most confident or reckless economic or social historian would hesitate at putting an exact date on when one 'Age' ceased and a new one started. This suggests that change is, and always has been, a continuous process. So, there were elements of the information age during the industrial age, and vice versa.

The discussion so far allows us to underline a very important feature of change. It is *not new*. We have always had it and will continue to do so. Learning how to manage change effectively therefore may be helped by briefly examining our current knowledge and experience of change which will, at the very least, extend our understanding of the nature of change itself. I shall do this by exploring how change operates on species, on individuals and on organizations.

CHANGE AS EXPERIENCED BY SPECIES

One change phenomenon that most of us are familiar with is the evolution of living organisms in the form of different species. The theory of natural selection expounded by Charles Darwin, while not without controversy, is now widely accepted as an explanation of this process (Ardrey, 1967, 1970, 1977). Essentially, the theory suggests that species need to adapt and change to changing physical environments if they are to survive. Those species that do adapt and change survive and prosper; those that stay the same become extinct. An interesting feature of the theory of natural selection is that it operates at two levels; 'inter' and 'intra' species. In practice, this means that individual members of a species with features or characteristics providing selective advantage successfully reproduce and thus ensure those features are passed on to give primacy in the survival stakes with other competing species.

Evolution is a continuous and ongoing process. There are many high profile campaigns to save this or that life form which provide testimony to that statement. In fact, the campaigns not withstanding, there are species of plants and animals existing as I write these words which will be extinct by the time you read them. We sometimes forget that the species homo sapiens is also evolving and continuously changing. Physical features such as average height, weight and life span are perhaps the most obvious example of changes that have occurred and are occurring, but intellectual and emotional characteristics are changing too. On any comparison, human beings are not the same today as when we first emerged as an identifiable species, nor will we be the same in 5,000 or 10,000 years time.

The process of evolution, however, does not imply a one way chain of cause and effect between environment and species. The science of ecology teaches us that there exists a set or series of mutually dependent relationships among the various life forms on the planet. This idea leads to the suggestion that species interact with, influence and change their environments. Instead of being passive responders and adaptors, life forms engage in symbiotic relationships with their environment. It is through this interaction that natural selection works to determine survival or extinction.

If at this point you are wondering about the relevance of this to this book, I invite you to do two things. First, think about the assumptions and arguments that underpin the theory of natural selection and compare them with the dimensions suggested by Wilson described in the opening paragraph. Second, compare them with the rationale presented to justify any major change recently undertaken in your own organization. We will return to the application of the ideas later in the chapter.

CHANGE AS EXPERIENCED BY INDIVIDUALS

As well as species as types of life forms, each individual living organism is subject to a process of change. This process is normally characterized as a life cycle consisting of birth, growth, development, decline and death. This cycle applies irrespective of which species is being examined.

If we examine ourselves we know that each of us has changed as individuals. Our physical characteristics are the most easily observable changes, but we also change intellectually and emotionally as we go through our lives. However, these changes do not, as we sometimes assume, end with maturity; they continue throughout life. Three examples will illustrate the point. Physically, everyone who reaches an average life span will be shorter in height at death than the maximum reached sometime earlier in their lives. Intellectually, it is the case that cognitive skills such as retaining and recalling information are different at the ages of 2, 20 and 60 years. Emotionally, the sound of a baby crying will evoke different feelings and behavioural responses at 3, 30 or 70 years of age. However, while the *fact* of change is common, the *nature* of the change will of course vary between individuals. Development can take us in all sorts of different directions.

Two other features are true of individual change among homo sapiens. First, a significant influence on development is the environment. In its broadest sense, our environment provides much of the experience which influences our physical, intellectual and emotional development. My personal belief, in terms of the nature versus nurture debate, is that we are born with biologically determined propensities and potentialities which operate in general directions at the level of the species. It is, in my view, the interaction of a unique set of life experiences with an equally unique biological potential that ultimately shapes the development of an individual. However, the individual is not a passive responder to their life experience and equally helps to shape their environment. So, the second feature is that, as sapient beings, individuals are capable of exercising free will and independent choice and therefore are inextricably involved in determining their own development.

This last point reflects what I believe to be two truths about our personal and individual environments. First, a significant feature of our experience is the 'social environment' in which we develop, ie, the other individuals with whom we regularly interact. The social environment can be constituted at various levels, for example, society, community, family or work organization. Second, we ourselves form part of the social environment for those other individuals; so, in a sense, we also constitute the 'social environment'. Therefore, as with species, individuals also influence and shape their environment.

There is one final significant factor concerning individual change. It is perhaps the most important of all, certainly for the arguments presented in this book. Development and change to do with intellectual and emotional characteristics occur through *learning* and, at the level of the individual, these three words can almost be used synonymously. There is a link here also with the previous section on species. A species has an increased chance of survival if its individual members are able to adapt their behaviour in response to a changing environment. This individual ability to adapt is often claimed to be the reason for the success of our species; our greatest strength as a species is our individual ability to learn. I will examine how the process of learning operates in later chapters. The important point here is to accept that learning is the key to individual change.

CHANGE AS EXPERIENCED BY ORGANIZATIONS

We come now to the relevance of this examination of change, as experienced by species and individuals, to the management of change in organizations. There are at least three points of interest. First, there are many potential lessons in nature for all aspects of human existence. A simple illustration of this point comes from architecture and the design of all types of physical structures. Many of the principles which underpin structural design can be found in and are derived from natural forms that exist in the living world, eg, the load bearing properties of a spider's web. The second point of interest is the simple truism that work organizations are literally 'peopled' by individual members of the human species. We cannot understand organizations without first understanding human beings. Nor can we hope to manage organization change without that understanding. The third point is that changes as experienced by species and individuals provide the rationale for, or are paralleled by, various explanations and models of organization change. Before examining some of these and associated approaches to managing change in more detail, the following list summarizes some of the key points that emerge from our analysis of change among species and individuals.

- Change is a natural phenomenon.
- Change is continuous and ongoing.
- The purpose of change is to aid survival and growth.
- Survival and growth are dependent upon adaptation to a changing environment.
- The environment can be and is influenced and shaped by the decisions and actions of the organization.
- Learning from experience is essential for successful adaption and change.
- Individuals and organizations change in both common and unique directions.

This list, in part, provides a rationale for an analytical model I have developed to help focus attention on *exactly* what change or changes are being managed. It seems to me that one of the confusions in thinking about managing change is a lack of precision in specifying 'the what' of change management. The model is intended to provide help in gaining that precision.

The model suggests two key dimensions, each of which can have two broad possibilities. The first dimension focuses on the *location* of change. Thus, we can attempt to manage either external change or internal change. What constitutes managing change will be different in each case. This point also applies to the second dimension which is to do with the cause or intent associated with the change. Again, there are two possibilities. The change can be deliberate, intended, or desired, ie, *planned*. Alternatively, the change may be unintended or unplanned: rather, it arises out of the nature of the world, and therefore is dynamic. The simple distinction here is between change which is intended and change which is not. Combining the two

Dimension of source/location

		Internal	External
Dimension of reason/cause	*Planned*	Quadrant A	Quadrant B
	Dynamic	Quadrant C	Quadrant D

Figure 2.1   *Management of Change: key dimensions*

dimensions provides four possible categories of change as illustrated in Figure 2.1.

Some examples may help to illustrate the meaning and application of the model. Implementing a new policy and system on, for example, staff appraisal is both *internal* and *planned*. The unpredictable vagaries of turnover of key staff is similarly internal but, because there is a lack of organizational intent, it is *dynamic*. A piece of government legislation is clearly *planned*, since the government intends it, but it is equally clearly *external*, since the change happens outside the organization. Conversely, the changing profile of the population caused by, or reflected in, demographic trends is similarly external though unintended by anyone and therefore *dynamic*. These examples also illustrate the earlier point that organizational decisions and actions intended to manage these changes will be different in each case. Managing planned change, whether decided internally or imposed externally, is, generally, a matter of applying principles governing change processes over a given time period (see next chapter). However, managing dynamic change is more to do with the nature of the organization's style and culture. Some organization forms are likely to be more effective than others in having the flexibility and adaptiveness to respond to dynamic change (see Chapters 4 and 6).

Environmental determinism

The model in Figure 2.1 includes the significant role of the environment in organization change. This reflects a number of theories of organization change which can be categorized under the label 'environmental determinism'. These theories hold the common view that organizations are subject to the demands of their environments, and that their success or otherwise is a result of their ability to meet those demands. This reflects one of Wilson's dimensions mentioned earlier. One particular set of these theories is that known as 'Population Ecology' (Tushman and Romanelli, 1985). The arguments in these models are very similar to those underpinning Darwin's theory of natural selection.

Whether or not we accept the absolute determinism of population ecology, it is the case that organizations cannot ignore their environment. They need to adapt to changing environments which requires, as with individuals, learning the intellectual and emotional lessons of experience. It

Social   -   eg   Demographic features such as age profiles, birth
                          rates, education levels, size of social classes.
                          Social norms and expectations such as dress, hous-
                          ing, standard of living, treatment of minorities, care
                          of sick and elderly, patterns of speech and relation-
                          ships.

Technological -   eg   New raw or synthetic materials.
                          New equipment and machinery.
                          New systems and/or processes.
                          Inventions.

Economic   -   eg   Macro-level such as interest rates, currency ex-
                          change rates, fiscal policies, labour market variables.
                          Micro-level such as market size and demand, com-
                          petitors, costs of production, local labour market
                          variables.

Political   -   eg   National and international laws, statutory regulations
                          and codes, relations between countries, pressure
                          groups, political parties and systems.

Figure 2.2   *STEP analysis*

also requires being aware of and taking account of the impact and effects of organization actions on the environment.

That last point to some extent reflects popular usage of the word 'environment' to imply the physical and natural environment which constitutes the total planet. This is obviously an important feature but it is not the only one. The extent of the external factors which create the need for organization change is neatly summarized in the concept of the 'operating environment'. What this means is simply all of those elements, sometimes referred to as direct and indirect, which affect and influence organization survival and growth. One way of analysing the direct elements is through stakeholder analysis. This involves specifying all of those groups who have a legitimate interest, or 'stake', in the success of the organization (eg, staff, shareholders, customers, suppliers) and determining their needs and wants from the organization. Indirect elements can be examined through application of STEP analysis. The meaning and application of this technique is illustrated in Figure 2.2.

Regular and intelligent application of stakeholder and STEP analysis enables organizations to identify what is happening and changing in their operating environment and to determine and implement appropriate responses, ie, adapt for survival and growth.

Internal factors

An organization's response to a changed environment requires internal change. This is implied to some extent in the model in Figure 2.1. Internal change is also the major focus of some alternative theories, other than environmental determinism (Tushman and Romanelli, 1985). For instance, those theories that apply the principles of individual change to underpin 'life cycle' models of organization change.

Irrespective of such responsive changes, there are also forces for change operating in organizations. These forces may or may not support required responses. In any case, they too require managing. They constitute the dynamic changes indicated in Figure 2.1. A list of what might constitute such forces is given below.

- Key personnel; eg, a new Chief Executive or other senior manager.
- Trade unions; eg, Becoming unionized or deunionized. Changes in personnel and/or policies and/or power of established unions.
- Performance; eg, Increases or decreases will affect size, confidence, morale.

- Motivation; eg, Groups or individuals working with more or less effort. Can be influenced by other forces.
- Group relationships; eg, The level, content and patterns of communication between different divisions or departments.
- Individual relationships; eg The personal relationship enjoyed by two individuals. Particularly significant at senior manager level

External and internal change

We can conclude from this analysis that organizations face two sets of demands if they are to survive and grow: the external and internal forces for change. The key task for managers then is to manage responses to these two sets of forces. This requirement is neatly summarized in a phrase from Schein (1988) who argues that organizations continuously have to achieve 'external adaptation and internal integration'. The purpose and focus of efforts to do so are, in a nutshell, what managing change is all about. The need for working at internal integration arises from the diversity of human individuals. It is also the purpose of currently fashionable culture management programmes (Anthony, 1994). Variation in personal values and beliefs is likely to be present in an organization at any given point in time. Some will be consistent and some inconsistent with desired or required change to meet the demands of the external environment. Managing change in this respect means directing the energy and behaviour of as many individual organization members as possible towards the desired direction and doing so in the fluid context and complexity of such energy and behaviour which constitutes real organization life.

SO WHAT'S NEW?

The demands described in this chapter have been faced by work organizations for as long as they have existed. Indeed, it could be argued that the demands represent the dilemma successfully managed to date by homo sapiens as a species. Our success as a species derives in part from inherent characteristics, such as a biological propensity to form groups, to work cooperatively and to learn from experience. Such characteristics also provide a basis for the success of organizations, although the seeds of decline can also lie in the same features.

There is, however, something new in human experience. It is what explains the contemporary interest in change management. What is new is quite simply the *rate* and *speed* of change, together with its growing *complexity.* Advances in technology are an often quoted example, though there are others. Political change in Central and Eastern Europe and the emergence of newly industrialized nations in the Far East, South America and Africa are other examples. These changes are not unconnected. For example, communications technology available now means that currency transactions that used to take hours, or even days, can now be completed in seconds. The effects of this on national economies and industrial and commercial organizations is, as yet, little understood.

One of the best known and most influential writers on the phenomenon is Alvin Toffler. His work and our own experience suggest that the biggest challenge facing the world is change itself. It is not any particular or specific change that we have to respond to, but living with complex change as a way of life. That is the challenge facing work organizations as we prepare for the end of the twentieth century and the beginning of the next. Like any other organization function, training and development has to offer a contribution to meeting that challenge. The rest of the book offers some ideas on how that can be achieved.

3. Planned organization change

Many writers on management have recognized the similarities of experience between organizations and the individuals who inhabit them. One famous example of this is the differentiation between 'mechanistic' and 'organic' organizational forms offered by Burns and Stalker (Burns, 1966). The previous chapter has suggested, however, that all organizations share certain properties in common with species and individuals. The idea of an organization 'life cycle' is one illustration of these properties which is now a well established concept in the management literature. The basic proposition of the concept is that organizations, like individuals, experience certain defined and identifiable stages.

While it is the case for individuals, there is no necessary requirement for the latter two stages to occur for species or organizations. This is especially the case where the capacity to learn from experience and continuously adapt to change is present. So long as *homo sapiens* as a species continues to utilize that capacity then our future looks assured (notwithstanding the possibilities of the destruction of the planet through nuclear disaster or the effects of the abuse of the physical and natural environment). The same is true of organizations. There is no necessary condition of nature that determines organizations will eventually die.

Indeed, organizations can be said to share a further property in common with species and individuals and that is an inherent desire to survive and grow. That this is the case can again be evidenced by a common-sense analysis of personal experience. But, as we have already seen, survival and growth require that change is managed. The essence of managing change is to achieve beneficial outcomes for the organization from the external and internal sources of change. Only then can the organization achieve its desire for survival and growth.

This chapter and the three that follow examine a variety of approaches and methods for effectively managing change. What these approaches and methods have in common is that they are appropriate for use when managing change across and throughout the totality of the organization, ie, the change will have implications for all organization members or a

significant group within the organization. There are, however, two important caveats to this generalization. The first is that there are important links
between the three levels of organization, group/team and individual. The
second is that the term 'organization' does not necessarily apply to the
totality of the corporate entity. The concept of organization can be applied
to a particular division or department or section of a wider organizational
entity. The same principles apply.

We are however concerned first with managing change at the level of the
organization and we begin in this chapter by exploring the concept of
planned change.

A DEFINITION AND EXPLORATION OF PLANNED CHANGE

Before describing and examining the theory and practice of planned change
we need to reach an understanding of the concepts implicit in the term.
Change requires that 'things' become different. This may seem a simple and
obvious statement but it forces us to further helpful conclusions. In order for
change to have happened we must know that 'things' are different. This
means that we must be able to measure and/or observe the difference
between a present and future or past state. Therefore, planned change is to
do with factors that are measurable or observable. Without that condition,
planned organization change is inconceivable. The kind of factors at the
organizational level therefore that we are interested in are 'things' like size,
performance, structure, policies, procedures, culture and management style.
Some of these are easier to observe or measure than others, for example size
and performance as opposed to culture and management style. However, if
we are to deal seriously with managing organization change we must know
what is the present state, what we want it to be, how progress will be
monitored and how we will know when change has been achieved. This
inevitably requires observable and measurable factors. Difficult as it may be,
the attempt at least must be made.

Organizations can and do change through a 'natural' process of
development. Any organization will be different 10 years from now whether
it desired and planned to change or, conversely, was unaware of change
taking place. These changes will be observable and measurable. *Planned*
change implies a conscious and positive decision to bring about a desired
difference. Therefore, planned change is to do with the implementation of a
specific decision in order to overcome a 'felt' need or problem. The felt need

or problem may itself derive from a change in the operating environment or from an internal source. As a useful starting point in examining this practice, we begin with a model of the planned change process.

A CHANGE PROCESS

Any change process can be seen to involve a series of identifiable stages. There are many such theories and models in the literature, some complex, others simple (Tushman and Romanelli, 1985). One which I believe to have much to commend it since it has great practical utility was originally devised by Hinings (1983). This model has five stages:

1. Diagnosis.
2. Identifying resistance.
3. Allocating responsibility.
4. Developing and implementing strategies.
5. Monitoring.

Before examining the application of the model in more detail one very important feature of this change process needs to be underlined. All of the theories and models of change developed by researchers and academics seem to have one thing is common. This is an emphasis on the interrelationships and interactiveness between the different stages that can be distinguished and labelled. This is also true of Hinings' model. Organization life is messy and attempts to manage organization change perhaps even more so. It is simply not possible to systematically carry out a logical series of activities in the linear manner implied by Hinings' five stages.

The reason for this is best illustrated by part of a novel I read a number of years ago. *The Fifth Horseman* is a political thriller and the plot concerns an atomic bomb being placed in New York by a group of terrorists who proceed to blackmail the government of the USA. One response by the authorities dealing with the crisis is to consider evacuating New York. The person in the federal government responsible for coordinating the activity is dispatched from Washington to discuss the idea with the New York Crisis Committee. This official had spent about 30 years of his career preparing plans for the evacuation of all of America's major cities with a major allocation of his time being devoted to New York. The plan he presented to the Committee ran to about seven volumes and was extremely impressive in its analysis of available transport resources linked to population numbers and final safe destinations. The only form of transport concluded as being feasible by the report was the subway system. The final parts of the plan gave all the necessary details of requirements for trains and carriages, number of journeys, departure times and locations, etc to provide safe evacuation for all New Yorkers within a given time-scale. In fact the plan was so comprehensive and detailed in every respect that the Crisis Committee were unanimous in the view that it was, as a plan, as near perfect as possible. They were also unanimous in the view that it wouldn't work! You might well anticipate the reason but it was left to the New York Police Commissioner to explain why to the distraught Washington official. He did this by posing the very simple question 'Who will drive the (expletive deleted) trains?'

The question nicely illustrates the fact that the evacuation planner had not considered the effects on the individual New Yorker of an announcement to evacuate the city; in simple terms he had forgotten the 'human factor'. A similar and reinforcing point was made by Sir John Harvey-Jones, the ex-Chairman of ICI, at a conference I attended on Strategic Management in late 1990. Sir John was speaking about strategic plans formulated in ICI which were equally impressive to that of the Washington planner but never actually worked in practice. This was for two reasons. First, such plans can never accurately anticipate and 'budget' for the response of individual human beings. Second, such plans, almost by definition, are also never likely to inspire the human spirit.

Hinings himself recognizes the point and emphasizes that the five stages should not be seen as separate or free-standing. Instead, planned change needs to be seen as an iterative process. That is, the stages should be seen as a series of 'steps' and, like footsteps, they can be taken backwards and sideways as well as forwards. In reality, the stages will be interwoven into the fabric of the change process and will occur in varying orders with some running concurrently and with many retreats into 'previous' stages. It is also almost impossible in practice to identify when one stage ends and another begins. What is of critical importance is to recognize that for planned change to be effective each stage needs to occur, and that the way each stage is managed needs to ensure that they are mutually supportive and reinforcing. Having reached that understanding we can now examine the model in more detail.

The process examined

1. Diagnosis
Being in some senses a starting point and being concerned with determining exactly what change is required or desired, it is critical that sufficient time

and attention is devoted to activities in this stage. It is often missed or done badly in work organizations and poor results are almost guaranteed to ensure that the other stages in the process will not be successful. The consequence of this is obviously that the planned change either fails to materialize or produces detrimental outcomes.

The basic purpose of the diagnostic stage is to reach a clear understanding of the felt need or problem. It involves examining the need or problem in as much detail as possible in order to establish clarity. The basic activities are those of data collection and analysis. What form those activities will take will depend on a number of factors including the nature of the problem or need and whether it is the result of an external or internal source of change. In many cases, the diagnostic stage will involve internal data collection, irrespective of the location of the source, and therefore will involve overlap with Stage 2 in the process. If internal data collection activities involve wide consultation with those affected by the change then overlap with Stage 4 will also occur. These two examples of overlap illustrate the iterative nature of the process.

2. *Identifying resistance*

As the story from *The Fifth Horseman* illustrates, individuals may not necessarily be in favour of a given course of action. It is again part of our own experience that this is the case. My own view is that people's natural resistance to change is sometimes overstated, if it is true at all. As human beings we have a propensity to learn from experience and to adapt our behaviour so I am unsure if there is such a phenomenon as *natural* resistance to change. The basic lesson of evolution though is that change is judged in terms of its effectiveness in aiding survival and growth. While this concept is not wholly applicable to individual responses to change, it does suggest a useful principle of positive benefits. That is, individuals are unlikely to favour a change unless they perceive it to be attractive and beneficial. It is obviously important to be aware of where resistance is likely to occur as part of managing a planned change. That is the purpose of this stage.

Hinings' work provides a second and very useful model (Figure 3.1) to illustrate the impact of agreement, or otherwise, to change on the success of a given planned change effort.

Figure 3.1 provides us with a number of useful indicators. First, it suggests that a given planned change is unlikely to be successful if those affected by it do not agree that a problem or need exists. The consequent resistance is likely to be greater in circumstances where those affected also disagree that the proposed solution, ie, the change itself, would be appropriate even if they

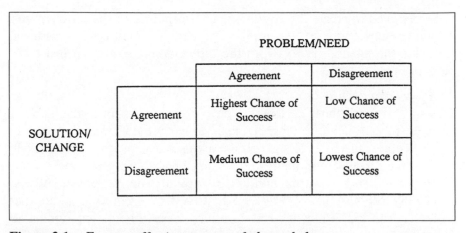

Figure 3.1 *Factors affecting success of planned change*
(Source: Hinings, 1983*)*

accepted that the need existed. This is illustrated in the bottom right hand quadrant. The second useful indication is the circumstances that need to exist or be created if a planned change is to be successful. The top left quadrant represents those circumstances, ie, that those affected agree with both the need to change and the particular change being proposed. Finally, the model indicates through the bottom left quadrant that as a minimum requirement for a reasonable chance of success those affected by a planned change need to accept that a need or problem exists which requires some change. In summary, Figure 3.1 provides a clear representation that change required of individuals needs to be perceived as offering positive benefits to them for it to be embraced.

The model also allows us to reach two further conclusions. First, that in circumstances represented by the bottom right quadrant, greater time and effort are likely to be required to implement a given change successfully. Second, that the time and effort expended should be directed at achieving the conditions represented in the top left quadrant, ie, shifting those affected by the change 'diagonally' through the model.

Stage 2 of the planned change process is about establishing the position of the organization in terms of Hinings' model. It involves identifying who will be affected by the change, how they are likely to perceive it, whether and to what extent they will resist and, critically, why they are likely to resist. Such an analysis is necessary for reaching appropriate decisions in the next two stages. It is particularly significant for Stage 4 since implementation strategies need to reflect the significance of the change for those affected and to be designed to create the conditions of acceptance of the problem and solution. Steps taken to accomplish the task of identifying resistance, reflecting the relationship between the different stages, may in fact form parts of Stages 3 and 4.

3. Allocating responsibility

This stage is particularly designed to develop commitment to the planned change. It means appointing individuals to carry the change through, ie, giving people leadership roles in managing the change process. This is likely to build their own commitment to the change and to provide a motivation for them to work towards building the same commitment in others. Allocating responsibility also reflects the truism of organizational life that without clear indications of responsibility tasks do not get done and decisions do not get made. This point also illustrates the need as part of this stage to go further than simply allocating leadership roles. In some circumstances it may be necessary to review and amend the job description of groups of staff in the organization and to build in new or revised responsibilities related to the planned change. This of itself may not achieve success but it may be a necessary condition.

The primary activity of the third stage is allocating leadership roles. The choice of who should have these roles and how they will be exercised is not straightforward. As with other stages, decisions will depend on the nature and source of the change. Such decisions also need to be consistent with and supportive of decisions and activities in the other stages. What is clear from academic enquiry and practical experience is that such roles should not necessarily be confined to those with established managerial positions nor that they should be exercised through an individual's formal authority. The literature on the use of Quality Circles and other forms of project groups bear testament to the validity of this point. Perhaps the most critical factors to take into account in allocating responsibility are the locations and extent of likely resistance and the form of the implementation strategy.

4. Developing and implementing strategies

This stage is concerned with implementing the planned change. It is important to understand at this point that this does not necessarily mean that all decisions have been taken. Decision makers at the top level in work organizations may believe that they know best and have the right to determine what will change. We know from Figure 3.1, however, that this does not mean that their decisions will necessarily be implemented in practice or that beneficial results will be achieved. The primary purpose of Stage 4 in the planned change process is to ensure an effective organization response to the felt need or problem and this requires the response to have the support of organization members. Stage 4 is about ensuring that the circumstances represented in the top left quadrant of Figure 3.1 exist or are created.

There are two sets of ideas that I have found of practical value in developing and implementing a change strategy. The first was originally devised as a result of research to help bring about change in the farming industry in the UK. The basic idea is illustrated in Figure 3.2.

The normal distribution curve in the figure suggests that within any given population affected by a change there will be a small number of 'innovators' who will welcome and embrace the change almost immediately and a similar small number of 'laggards' who will resist the change to the last and may never adopt it. In between the two extremes will lie the majority of the population who will broadly fall into two camps; those who are likely to adopt the change quite quickly and those who will take longer and/or more convincing. These two groups are usually referred to as either 'early adopters' or 'late adopters'. I use the expression 'the change' quite deliberately. While it might well be the case that individuals differ in broad personality terms in their propensity to welcome or resist change *per se*, even if this personality factor were known for the entire population affected by a given change it would not give a firm guide as to who will be innovators and

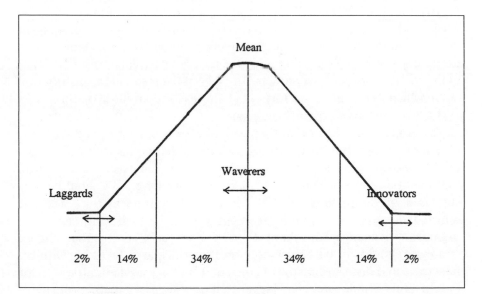

Figure 3.2 *Innovators and laggards*

who laggards. This is because individuals judge each proposed change on its own merits and a person whose personality assessment and general behaviour indicates an 'innovator' may in fact take the approach of a 'laggard' in relation to a particular change that is disagreed with, and vice versa – a general 'laggard' can be an 'innovator' in relation to a specific change. Nor is job or occupation or position in the organization hierarchy a useful indicator. The innovators and laggards have to be identified for each planned change and identified as individuals. A final point about Figure 3.2 needs to be made. It is unlikely that the distribution of the population will form a normal curve. In reality the curve is likely to be skewed in one direction or the other, and the amount of skew and direction will vary according to the nature and source of each change.

Figure 3.2 does, however, provide some useful guidelines on implementing planned change. It tells us that there will be innovators and laggards. This is useful to know. It also indicates that these are generally likely to be minorities in the total population and that a significant proportion of the majority will 'lean' in the direction of adopting the change. This also can be useful and reassuring. It is also the case that innovators can be highly effective in influencing others to adopt change. This can be in a passive way such as being significant as a 'reference group' or 'model' which others seek to emulate, and where benefit is achieved by innovators who can provide evidence and powerful argument to persuade others to adopt the change. Innovators, once identified, can also be used actively to influence others. They can be allocated leadership roles as part of Stage 3 of the process. In doing so, they are encouraged to actively promote and persuade and so exercise a positive influence on others. Such activity will be very significant in the speed of adoption of those to the right of the mean in the distribution curve which itself will have a form of chain reaction on those on both right and left of the curve close to the mean.

The model also tells us that there will always be laggards, and that they may never adopt the change. In organizational terms this means that they might choose or be required to leave. Knowing of their existence does mean that realistic targets can be set for implementing change. We should not be surprised or disappointed if 100 per cent commitment from everyone affected does not materialize. It is always likely to be the case. One organization change consultant I know once advised me that change strategies should always be designed on the principle of 'working with the new wave and disregarding the old guard'. I find this advice a little extreme but, in terms of innovators and laggards, it does suggest a useful principle of not wasting time and effort on individuals or groups who are definitely going to resist to the last and perhaps not change at all. It is, though, sometimes useful to attempt to convert a small number of laggards to innovators as part of the implementation strategy, especially if they occupy positions of power and influence. This is particularly useful since laggards are likely to be highly committed to their position, and will therefore seek to influence others.

The idea of innovators and laggards provides a useful principle for developing and implementing a change strategy. It is to maximize the influence and impact of innovators and to minimize the effects of the laggards. There is another general principle which is equally useful, supported by much evidence in social science theory and research. It is simply that the key to converting laggards and waverers to innovators is *involvement*. This principle is also the most effective way to ensure that the conditions represented by the ideal quadrant in Figure 3.1 will exist in relation to any given planned change.

The application of this principle is widespread in organization and management theory. It forms the basis of many models of effective management style and successful leadership behaviour. It is also implicit in many theories of effective teamwork and organization change. The principle has stood the test of time and keeps appearing in different guises in 'new' advice to managers on how to be successful. However, its application in developing a strategy for organization change does not always mean literal involvement by all those affected. There are a range of possible strategies for implementing change which can be rated according to the degree of involvement. This range is similar in many respects to well known and established theories of 'a management style continuum'. My own conceptualization of this idea as it applies to strategies for planned change is given in Figure 3.3.

In developing and implementing a strategy for planned change a choice needs to be made on the extent to which to involve those affected by the change. At one extreme people are merely told of the change and expected to adopt it. This is labelled an *information* strategy, ie, information about the change is passed on without the opportunity or expectation of a response, apart from adopting the change. At the other extreme all (or nearly all) those affected are fully involved in the identification of the need or problem and determination of the solution. This is termed an *involvement* strategy. In between are a number of possibilities which vary according to the degree of interaction between decision makers and those affected, and the relative degree of influence on decisions by the same two groups.

The principle discussed earlier would suggest that high involvement is a necessary strategy. I agree with the idea as a *general* principle but it is not always true in practice. For example, there are clearly some planned changes such as reducing a workforce through redundancy which are unlikely to gain the agreement of all those affected. Conversely, some changes are so insignificant in their impact on those affected that the vast majority will accept and support them without dissent, for example the adoption of a new corporate identity and logo. Even so, these examples do illustrate the utility of Figure 3.3 and the general principle. Some degree of involvement at the level of *consultation* or *negotiation* is likely to minimize the detrimental consequences of the change for those affected and the rest of the organization in the first case, and some level of involvement may produce

LOW INVOLVEMENT

Information	eg	Written materials such as memos, revised policy statements, circulars, staff magazines, posters. Face-to-face meetings such as staff conferences, presentations and `launches'. Use of in-house videos.
Communication	eg	Small group meetings such as team briefings where staff affected may ask questions and have them answered.
Consultation	eg	Questionnaire and attitude surveys. Small group briefing sessions. Use of formal systems and procedures such as staff association committees.
Negotiation	eg	Use of elected or nominated staff respresentatives. Formal systems and procedures such as Trade Union or Staff Association joint committees.
Participation	eg	Single or multi-functional working parties and project groups.
Involvement	eg	Organization-wide and department/section-based task groups with multi-functional and multi-level membership. Quality circles.

HIGH INVOLVEMENT

Figure 3.3 *A continuum of implementation strategies*

much better results at much lower costs than a high flying PR consultancy in the second example. It remains the case, however, that on occasions a straightforward information strategy may be appropriate.

Application and use of Figure 3.3 is in terms of making choices on what type of strategy to adopt in Stage 4 of the planned change process. The choice, like so many others, will depend on the nature of the particular change. As a general rule, the more significant the change and its impact, as perceived by those affected, the higher the degree of involvement required for success. The ideas expressed in Figure 3.3 can also be used in conjunction with those in Figure 3.2, and can also take advantage of the iterative nature of the whole process. For instance, where a consultation or negotiation level strategy is adopted then innovators can be used as staff representatives. Conversely, it may be wise to use some laggards as a means of converting them to innovators. Even at the level of information or communication, innovators can be consciously used to convey the message or be used as examples of success in the message. Some elements of these strategies can also be useful in applying Stage 3 of the process, ie, allocating responsibility. Formation of working parties and task groups can be based around particular areas of responsibility to do with the change. Allocation of leadership roles within such groups can be based on known innovators. Any element of all levels of strategy, including information and communication, can be useful in identifying resistance, ie, Stage 2 of the process. The two models in Figures 3.2 and 3.3 have wide utility throughout the process of planned change.

I have written at length about Stage 4 in the process because it is a stage in which there is a lot of scope for choice. The earlier stages are primarily concerned with information collection and analysis and, as we have seen, can be aided by developing and implementing an appropriate strategy. There is, though, a critical element to any change strategy that I have not yet mentioned and that is the provision of training and development. No strategy will work without it. I will, however, not deal with this part of the strategy here, as it is addressed in detail in later chapters, save for one piece of advice. In broad terms, the type of training and development activities provided need to reflect the type of strategy adopted as defined in Figure 3.3. As well as a need for consistency, it is also true that training and development is likely to be ineffective if it does not allow for an appropriate level of involvement.

5. Monitoring
This brings us to the final part of the process. It appears in some ways an

easy stage. What is required is the setting of targets, time-scales for achieving them, and setting up and applying the means to assess progress. Doing this in practice relies on Stage 1 being carried out thoroughly since implicit in monitoring is the need to describe the current position and future desired state. A clear picture of the present is necessary to assess progress towards the future. Also implicit in monitoring is the need for observable and measurable factors to be the focus of planned change. We cannot monitor what we cannot see or measure. The final part of the stage is an assessment of whether the planned change has been achieved and the felt need or problem overcome. But monitoring has to be carried out on a frequent and regular basis until that point, because this stage has a further key element. It is to do with identifying and dealing with unexpected outcomes. Plans and strategies do not always work as intended when put into action, so it is important to be able to respond to the actuality. This is a key purpose of monitoring. It also provides a final illustration of the iterative nature of the process. Unexpected and unintended consequences will mean reviewing and revising earlier stages, often including Stage 1.

A common result of monitoring, for example, is identifying resistance (Stage 2) in locations and for reasons impossible to anticipate with a consequent and necessary revision of the original rationale for the change (Stage 1). It is therefore an important stage which, like Stage 1, is too often ignored or done badly within work organizations. In fact, it is perhaps often the case that senior decision makers instigate a change without ever checking and therefore ever knowing whether it was implemented or achieved the desired effect, and then carry on doing their jobs in the belief that both have happened. Such behaviour can have detrimental and, on occasions literally disastrous, results for the organization and its members.

A change process in action

A recent example of planned change in action illustrates many of the principles discussed in the previous section.

CASE STUDY 1: ATLAS ENGINEERING

Atlas Engineering is a small family-owned engineering company employing approximately 500 staff. The product range is primarily aimed at car manufacturers. Competition was on the increase, especially from Japanese companies entering the market with great cost advantages and therefore significant price differentials. The Managing Director of the company decided that the processes currently used in manufacturing needed to change in order to reduce costs. This required many of the workforce to take on new and additional responsibilities to create a higher degree of flexibility in the use of labour and to produce greater efficiency. However, reorganization of the structure, responsibilities and tasks of the workforce was a sensitive issue given that Atlas was unionized and had a long history of traditional manufacturing processes and related roles for different categories of staff.

The Managing Director of Atlas sought to introduce the new processes simply by announcing his intention to operate them from a certain date and communicated the announcement through the management hierarchy. This method ignored nearly all of the stages of the planned change process and the Managing Director's plans were immediately resisted by the vast majority of the workforce. This resistance became a formal industrial relations issue which started along the road to becoming a major dispute. The commercial position of Atlas became even more threatened by the uncertainty and unrest within the organization caused by the resistance to the planned change.

This situation carried on in Atlas for a number of weeks with the Managing Director attempting to persuade union representatives of the need to change because of the Japanese competition. At one stage he even went on a fact-finding trip to Japan and brought back a report on the manufacturing processes used in that country which were a major reason for the price differentials. While this had some effect in persuading of the need to change, the resistance continued.

After two months of negotiating without success the Managing Director of Atlas decided on radical action. He proposed the formation of a Steering Committee within the organization to address the problem of increasing competition. His only insistence on its composition was that it should include members of staff from all levels and current functions as well as union representatives. The eventual size was 12, including managers, supervisors and operatives as well as full-time and part-time union officials, with the Managing Director chairing the committee. A visit to Japan for the full committee was also arranged.

The formation of the Committee and its visit to Japan had startling effects. All members came back from the trip totally persuaded of the need to institute change within Atlas and committed to finding and implementing appropriate solutions. The effect of being presented with evidence and arguments from their union representatives and work colleagues quickly persuaded the majority of the workforce to accept the need for change. However, the Steering Committee did not accept the Managing Director's original ideas on how the manufacturing process should change. Instead, they formed a series of project teams within the organization, again with membership drawn from all levels and functions, to examine and produce recommendations on new machinery, processes, structure, job definitions, etc. This work was completed in a very short time and resulted in a complete reorganization of the manufacturing department and supportive adjustments in other departments. Project teams worked in their own time as well as normal work hours and when the changes were implemented there was a high degree of commitment to make them work. The Steering Committee remained in existence to monitor implementation. It also eventually became a continuing and key part of the·management of the organization. Atlas was able to respond positively and competitively to the Japanese and continue to go from strength to strength. It has also through the experience increased its ability as an organization to utilize *planned change* as a means of ensuring beneficial results from inevitable change.

The story of Atlas is true. It is a real organization and went through the experience described. That experience is a useful demonstration of the value of the process of planned change. The Managing Director originally failed to apply any of the five stages effectively. His diagnosis (Stage 1) was limited to external factors and did not take account of the current situation within Atlas, eg, its history and traditions. While some resistance was expected, the extent and depth came as a surprise (Stage 2). Allocation of responsibility (Stage 3) was limited to the established management hierarchy, as was the simple information-based implementation strategy (Stage 4). There were no detailed arrangements for monitoring in his original plan apart from the expected improvement in efficiency (Stage 5). Perhaps by accident or force of circumstances the Managing Director eventually found an effective way to manage the change process. Application of the principles of planned change at the start would have saved the organization time, effort and money. If the Managing Director had not come to that application the consequences for Atlas could have been terminal.

SUMMARY

I do not intend to provide a full analysis of the application of the planned change process in Atlas Engineering. It seems to me possible to identify all five stages in the Managing Director's eventual actions and the application of the models in Figures 3.1 and 3.2. It also demonstrates the purpose of planned change: to ensure beneficial outcomes for the organization as illustrated in Figure 1.2 by managing the change processes. Planned change as a concept contains a set of ideas useful in managing organizations in a way which avoids the decline and death of nature's life cycle. The ultimate measure of managerial effectiveness is the avoidance of those stages. Awareness and application of the planned change process is therefore essential for competent management of a work organization.

The next chapter describes a further concept and related set of ideas for managing change at the organization level. The concept is organization development which has a close relationship with planned change.

4. Organization development

This chapter and the next examine a particular approach to organization change termed 'Organization Development' (OD). Our examination of OD will include looking at its origins and progress with some specific methods within the general approach, and a discussion of the practical application of the concepts in Chapter 5. Chapter 6 then turns to an examination of what might be termed the most recent articulation of OD; the idea of the learning organization. In Chapter 5 I will include some illustrative case studies drawn from my own experience of acting as an OD consultant. There are some important links between OD and the ideas contained in Chapter 3 on planned change, with which I will begin.

OD AND PLANNED CHANGE

Writers on management and organization behaviour tend to fall into two broad camps when considering OD and planned change. There are those who conceive of the two terms as being almost synonymous and interchangeable. For this group, OD is the only approach to planned change and planned change, by definition, consists of applying the tools and techniques of OD. The second group do not share this view and conceive of OD and planned change as being distinct and consisting of different ideas and concepts. There is, however, no large measure of agreement within this second group on what these distinctions are and a whole variety of distinguishing characteristics are discernible in the literature. This situation arising out of academic research and debate does not take us very far in reaching practical guidelines for managing change in work organizations. What is needed is a way of linking the two concepts together so that both can be usefully applied in practice.

Critical features of OD

OD in practice as a means of managing organization change is usually referred to as an 'OD effort' or 'OD programme'. These terms are part of the accepted jargon of OD and are used with equal comfort by both academics and practitioners. What they mean is quite simply carrying out a series of activities in order to change an organization. They are very similar in conception and practice to training and development, ie, carrying out a series of activities to change an individual. However, what these activities are designed to achieve in an OD programme is not just a desired response to a given change but the creation of a particular form of organization. It is important to be clear that it *does not* mean a form of organization *structure*. A particular 'form of organization' within the theory and practice of OD refers to a wide range of organizational characteristics being managed and operated in a certain manner. So, OD in theory and practice is not just about, and sometimes not at all about, managing a given change. It is essentially all about creating an organizational form which by its very nature is more capable of managing change itself. In that sense, OD is an approach to managing the natural development of an organization in a way which is more likely to achieve beneficial results, from external and internal sources of change and both planned and dynamic (see Figure 2.1) ie, creating an organization which is effective at managing change.

It is an implicit feature of OD that there exists an 'ideal' organization form and that the purpose of OD is to help its creation within a specific organization at specific times through OD efforts and programmes. It is debatable whether the 'ideal' organization exists in absolute terms which will apply in all cases although some OD writers and practitioners seem to believe that this is the case. It is more likely to be the case, in my view, that there are some useful general principles which need to find specific application in specific organizations and times. These general principles though are unlikely ever to encompass every aspect of organizational life and to apply equally to *all* organizations. What is important is that the theory and practice of OD have an implicit belief in an ideal organization form.

Relationship with planned change

This essential feature of OD seems to me to provide a key distinguishing feature from planned change. The latter is concerned with processes to adopt to manage change in response to specific needs or problems. OD on the other hand is about changing the organization in the direction of some conception of an ideal form irrespective of the existence of a given need or problem. The aim is to increase the organization's ability to manage change. If this distinction between the two concepts is accepted it then follows that OD and planned change are different and separate but that OD necessarily encompasses planned change. This is because OD is about moving the organization towards its ideal form which by definition means *changing* it, so it follows that the processes of planned change become relevant and, if they have any validity and value, probably essential. We can conclude from this that planned change will normally be a part of, a phase within, an OD programme. But, if OD and planned change are different and separate then each can exist and be applied without the other. In my experience this is in fact the case. As an organization member and consultant I have both witnessed and taken part in organization changes which applied the processes of planned change without any of the essential characteristics of an OD programme, including no vision of an ideal form outside of the desired change decided on as a response to the problem being tackled. Similarly, I have both witnessed and taken part in overtly identified OD programmes which had none of the features of planned change as part of their design. However, it is also my experience, which can find support in the literature, that OD programmes are likely to be more effective if they include a planned change phase as part of their design. My own conclusion on the links between OD and planned change, therefore, is that planned change can be usefully applied outside of OD programmes but that OD programmes should almost always include planned change.

OD DEFINED

OD is essentially a generic concept used to encompass a number of approaches and methods devised to improve organizational effectiveness. What these approaches and methods have in common and which also distinguishes them from alternatives is a concern to develop the organization into an effective learning system and to make effective organizational learning the essential method of managing change. This is perhaps the first and most important general principle describing the ideal organization form referred to earlier.

There are a number of formal definitions of OD to be found in the literature. The one given below captures for me the essential characteristics of OD theory and practice.

OD is the systematic and long-term application of behavioural science knowledge and theory as a means of improving organization effectiveness as measured by its ability to adapt its goals, structure, culture, style, etc in response to change.

A number of important ideas implicit in the definition require further explanation and discussion. This will hopefully bring more clarity and ease to an understanding of OD. Some illustrations of other views of OD later in the chapter will also help that process.

Systematic

The first term which requires examination is *systematic*. OD often has the image with managers of being a very unstructured and feelings-oriented approach and set of activities (Tyson and Jackson, 1992). This image is understandable since it is based on fact. Many of the tools and techniques of OD do have such characteristics. However, such methods should only be utilized as part of a planned and structured OD programme. Unfortunately, some OD practitioners often forget this and indulge in the use of methodologies and techniques solely for their own purposes and needs which unfortunately create a negative image. Professionally designed and delivered OD programmes may well use the same methods and techniques but only as part of an overall structure negotiated and agreed with managers. OD is and needs to be systematic if it is to be effective.

Long-term

As part of the systematic nature of OD, it is also a *long-term* process. Changing an organization towards some ideal form cannot be achieved overnight. Most OD programmes are over 12 months in length and a probable average would lie somewhere between three and five years. Just as there are no universal solutions so there are no immediate panaceas. OD requires a long-term investment in order to show results.

Behavioural science

A third idea in the definition worthy of further examination is *behavioural science*. This is a term which can, in my experience, cause some confusion. It seems that both academics and practitioners utilize different terminology in relation to the same subject and vice versa. Behavioural science is originally an American term. It can have at least three different meanings. The first makes it synonymous with psychology. The second refers to a particular school of thought within the discipline of psychology, ie, the Behaviourists. The third encompasses most if not all of the disciplines within science devoted to the study of human behaviour. This last meaning of behavioural science makes the term synonymous with what in the UK is usually called the social sciences. A study of the OD literature shows that this meaning is in fact the one implicit in OD. Therefore, within our definition, behavioural science refers to psychology, social psychology, sociology, anthropology, political science and the other social sciences including all their different branches and schools.

Effectiveness

The final term which needs explanation is *effectiveness*. A usual response to the idea of organization effectiveness would be to think about factors such as turnover and profit as commercial measures and budget size and number of employees and/or clients served as measures of effectiveness for not-for-profit organizations. In terms of OD, however, an effective organization is one which learns from experience and adapts to change. The ability to learn and change is the key measure of effectiveness. This ability may be more difficult to measure but it is the essential characteristic of the ideal organization. However, it is not pursued by OD as an end in itself. Rather, it is seen as a necessary pre-condition for survival, growth and improvements in the more usual measures of effectiveness such as turnover and profit. Creation of and/or improvements in the organization's ability to learn and change illustrates why OD is a long-term process.

Operating OD in practice

This discussion of my definition of OD points to the reasons why OD operates in the way it does and why it is of particular relevance to training and development practitioners and other HRM specialists. OD has been a growing force within HRM for over three decades and has been established as a relevant and useful approach for at least two of those. But it is still not as widely utilized as it could or should be. The reasons for this become clear if we look at how OD operates in practice.

Many large organizations employ OD specialists and these are usually located in separate OD departments. This is true on both sides of the Atlantic with OD departments being in existence in all sectors of the economy in both the USA and UK. Examples can be found in industrial and commercial organizations as well as public services such as the military, education and health. What is interesting is that in nearly all cases the OD department is *separated* from the mainstream organization structure and formal management hierarchy. It is also the case in both the USA and UK that much OD work is undertaken by external consultants. Many of the leading OD practitioners are academics working from universities and colleges or are independent consultants. Employed OD practitioners working from separate, 'stand alone' departments also usually operate on a consultancy basis with parts of or the whole of their parent organization. For some organizations this internal consultancy basis involves commercial fees. The essential feature of both external and internal consultants is that they are not directly employed by and accountable to their client managers outside of the terms of the particular consultancy contract. This existence of a contract between a client manager or group of managers and an OD consultant is the normal basis of operating an OD programme. The widespread use of internal and external consultants in OD programmes is simply because it is easier to change organizations by *working with* but not being *controlled by* the established power structures. And there lies the problem for employed HRM and training and development specialists.

Essentially, an OD consultant operates as a 'change agent', but this is also an expected and legitimate role for trainers and HRM specialists. There are two reasons why in practice this does not often happen and why therefore OD is not as widely utilized as it should be by organizations of all sizes. The first is a reluctance on the part of employed HRM and training specialists to confront and consciously manage the power structures and political realities of their organizations. The second is lack of knowledge and skill in utilizing behavioural science theory. Both reasons need to be addressed by trainers and HRM specialists. OD is an effective approach to managing change in organizations and HRM and training specialists cannot afford to ignore it if they are to remain relevant as an organization function. There are too few organizations large enough to justify separate OD departments and/or the fees of external consultants. There are also too many medium to small sized organizations facing turbulent change being denied required expertise for trainers and HRM specialists to avoid facing up to the challenge of OD.

Many OD specialists become so through an HRM or training route. This is to be expected because of all the organization functions these two are most likely to provide the opportunities, through professional education and experience, to acquire and develop the relevant skills. However, my view is that OD can, is and should be practised by training and development specialists as part of their repertoire of services and need not be left to either internal or external specialist practitioners.

THE NATURE OF OD

The nature of OD in practice is a little difficult to describe. All of the approaches and methods encompassed within OD accept three critical assumptions about organizations and organization change which in turn are derived from two key factors about life at the end of the twentieth century. The following description of the two factors and three assumptions will hopefully aid the description of OD itself.

The factor of human behaviour

The first factor is simply an increased and increasing understanding of human behaviour. We now know and understand more about why human beings behave as we do and this understanding is growing almost daily. It is not the purpose of this chapter nor even of this book to summarize that knowledge but a few examples will help to illustrate and reinforce the point. They will also illustrate the meaning of behavioural science referred to earlier.

Our increasing understanding operates at the level of the individual through advances in psychology, eg, motivation and learning theories; at the level of the group through social psychology and anthropology, eg, non-verbal behaviour and team skills; at the level of the organization through sociology and political science, eg, the connections between institutional structures and power relationships. All of these advances in the study of human behaviour reveal principles which can be usefully applied in managing organizations and organization change. They also inform and provide the basis of the assumptions which underpin OD.

The factor of change

The second factor has already been established in this book and it is the growing complexity of the operating environment facing all organizations. This factor simply recognizes that change is and will be the norm for organizations rather than the exception. Therefore, new 'ideal' organization forms are required.

Given those two factors, three assumptions seem both valid and critical.

The three assumptions of OD

Assumption 1 – Values
The theory and practice of OD assumes that humanistic values are relevant and required in work organizations of the future. This means viewing employees as thinking, feeling individuals with legitimate wants and expectations rather than as inanimate 'resources'. Such values are typically expressed by the Theory Y managers of Douglas McGregor's leadership

style continuum (see French, 1984). This set of values also underpins the belief that an individual's contribution can only be maximized by organizations through providing genuine opportunities for growth and development.

Assumption 2 – Process

OD is based on the premise that organizations need to learn. Often, the purpose of an OD programme is to help an organization to 'learn how to learn'. The OD process typically consists of a minimum of three stages: data gathering, diagnosis and active intervention. These stages roughly approximate the learning process of individuals.

Assumption 3 – Technology

This assumption is to do with accepting that organizations are living systems and therefore recognizing that intervening in one part will have effects and consequences for other parts and the whole. The 'technology' used, ie, the methods, tools and techniques utilized, must recognize the system nature of organizations and be capable of dealing with the total system.

These then are the guiding principles which underpin the theory and practice of organization development. I will give some indication of the range of methods and techniques used by OD practitioners in the next section. What is important to understand here is that OD as an approach to managing change rests on the three assumptions given above. Therefore, if you are engaged in some activity which reflects those assumptions you are practising OD. However, if you are engaged in an activity which utilizes one or more of the methods traditionally associated with OD, but in a way which does not reflect the assumptions then you are not practising OD. The distinction between what is OD and what isn't is that simple.

HISTORY AND PROGRESS OF OD

This last point and the nature of OD itself will perhaps become clearer through a review of the origins and progress of OD. This section will present a brief overview of the development of OD, drawing for the most part on Bennis (1969). Anyone interested in knowing more about the subject cannot do better than reading that book.

OD probably emerged as a separate academic discipline within the study of organizations and management sometime in the middle to late 1950s. It is difficult to be precise about the exact timing since it took a while for the coming together of disparate theories, models and methodologies into a cohesive and recognizable approach which incorporated a clearly sustainable set of principles. Since those early origins and reflecting its catholic nature, OD has continued to draw on research and theory from a wide range of disciplines within the social sciences.

Early focus

The early focus of OD was on changing organizations through changing the personal value systems of those who manage them. The major technology utilized for achieving that was the 'T' Group or sensitivity training. Thus, from the start OD had clear links with the training and development function and its practice required the same or similar skills. The use of this technology as a central part of the practice of OD grew out of the work of the National Training Laboratories (NTL) in America and the Tavistock Institute in the UK in the early 1950s. However, the approach and the technology are still seen as relevant in the 1990s; witness the still popular 'interpersonal skills' or 'personal growth' programmes for managers at all levels. These are the direct descendants of the NTL 'T' Group programmes. One of the most famous methods in OD is the Managerial Grid devised by Robert Blake and Jane Mouton. This methodology grew directly out of NTL 'T' Group methods and is still practised worldwide in the 1990s (see Chapter 5).

OD theories and methods

The continuing focus on personal values of managers provides an indication of a further characteristic of the 'ideal' organization implicit in OD. This is an organization and management style which reflects the humanistic values referred to earlier. A belief in the requirement of such values for achieving an effective organization also underpins the other major approaches to and methodologies of OD. Some of these methodologies and important theories which have been incorporated into OD practice over the last 25 years or so are summarized below.

Team development
There are now a variety of approaches to team development as a training and development activity. (These are explored in more detail in Chapter 9.) However, growing knowledge of group dynamics and the requirements for achieving effective teamwork led to team development activities being devised specifically for OD purposes. Two OD practitioners particularly associated with this approach are Mike Woodcock and Dave Francis who, both separately and in partnership, have published many books and articles

on the subject (eg, Woodcock, 1981). To illustrate and reinforce the point made earlier, team development of itself does not constitute OD. Only when it is practised in line with the three key assumptions listed in the previous section is team development an approach to OD.

Job design

Job design is a central part of HRM but, as with team development, it is not of itself OD. Techniques such as job enrichment and job enlargement, based on Hertzberg's work on theories of human motivation, can however be applied as an approach to OD (French, 1984; Stoner, 1989). Similarly, the design of jobs based on the principles of 'cellular production' can reflect the assumptions of OD and so be adopted as the basis of an OD programme. A famous example of this in practice is the Volvo auto production operation in Sweden. This was one of the first factories to create teams of workers responsible for discrete areas of work as an alternative to established assembly-line production.

Organization design

OD is about managing change in organizations. Two key questions implicit in that statement are, in what direction should the organization be changed, ie, what form of organization represents the ideal?; and what processes should be adopted to manage the transition, ie, how does the organization make the journey from the present state to the future state? There are now a number of related theories to do with organization design which can inform decisions on both questions and which therefore have been incorporated into OD practice. One is known as Systems Theory which simply suggests that organizations are living systems as we acknowledged earlier in describing the assumptions which underpin OD. The work of Cyert and March is useful in exploring this concept (French, 1984; Handy, 1985). A similar theory which grew out of research undertaken by Trist and Bamforth in the British coalfields is known as Socio-Technical Analysis (French, 1984; Wilson, 1990). This theory suggests that there are two major sub-systems in any organization: the 'technical' system by which the work is done and objectives achieved, and the 'social' system which involves the way individuals and groups in the organization relate to each other on an interpersonal level. According to this theory, designing an organization structure, and indeed designing individual jobs, requires both systems to be analysed and care taken to ensure compatibility between the two. Cellular production can be said to be an example of the application of this theory. A final set of theories are those which collectively represent what is known as the contingency approach to organization design. What these theories have in common is the notion that a given ideal organization form with general application does not exist and that the ideal form will vary from organization to organization depending on, or 'contingent' upon, certain factors. Views on what these factors are differ from researcher to researcher but generally encompass factors such as size, tradition and history, products, markets, production processes, amount of stability or change in the operating environment and the nature of the organization's core business. The major specific theories within the contingency approach can be found in the works of Lawrence and Lorch, Burns and Stalker, and Woodward (Burns, 1966; French, 1984; Handy, 1985; Wilson, 1990).

None of these theories on organization design represents OD. However, they can be and have been incorporated into the theory and practice of OD and have made a major contribution to its progress. For example, socio-technical analysis is a very useful tool in carrying out team development activities and, to some extent, it underpins the concept of the learning organization (see Chapter 6). The basic ideas of system theory and the contingency approach are highly relevant when embarking on an OD programme since they are very helpful in answering questions on both the destination and the 'method of transport' for the journey. The set of theories listed here are essential tools for the HRM specialist since the activity itself is a key part of the HRM function. Similarly, no training and development practitioner can afford to be ignorant of the theories if they are truly to be effective in helping to manage change.

Management and leadership style development

The personal values of individual managers have long been a focus of OD programmes. There are many theories of effective management style which underpin this approach. The drive for more participative management, which seems to be enjoying a renaissance in the 1990s, derives from the work of Lewin, Tannenbaun and Schmidt, and Argyris, among others (Bennis, 1976; French, 1984; Wilson, 1990). These writers tend to the view of their being one 'best' management style which is itself participative. Other researchers and writers on management take a view similar to those who promote the contingency approach to organization design in that the 'best' management style is seen as being dependent on surrounding, contextual factors. Some of the best known theorists who adopt this approach are Fiedler, Hearsey and Blanchard, and Reddin (French, 1984; Handy, 1985; Huczynski, 1987; Wilson, 1990). Again, there is disagreement on which factors are relevant or critical but they generally include the nature of the task or work and the nature of the team or individual being managed.

Again, none of these theories of themselves represent OD but they have been incorporated into its practice. Many OD programmes have as their underlying principle a particular theory of effective management style and the adoption of that style by the organization as their primary purpose. Many trainers are involved in management development programmes which provide examples of what I mean here. Providing the features of OD discussed earlier are present, then those trainers running such MD programmes are in effect practising OD. Conversely, where such programmes exist they present the opportunity for practising OD by the conscious and planned adoption of the underlying assumptions of OD in the design and delivery of the programme. This point provides further evidence of the importance of a sound understanding of OD theory and practice on the part of HRM and HRD specialists.

Management and leadership style provides an interesting example of the development of OD. There are in the 1990s many alternative approaches to management and leadership development available to the OD practitioner: use of outdoor activities such as abseiling, orienteering, raft-building, pot-holing, etc, and 'high-tech' methods such as interactive video are two examples. However, the underlying theories seem to me to be the same as or similar to those of the NTL 'T' Groups in the late 1950s. The validity of these theories seems to have been acknowledged with the endorsement by the Confederation of British Industry and others of the principles of management espoused by the UK-based Management Charter Initiative. The point about 'new' methodologies emerging which are based on 'old' theories could also be made about other aspects of OD.

Industrial democracy
This final example of approaches to OD developed over the years also illustrates the 'old' and the 'new' nature of OD. The European Union policy expressed in the Social Chapter illustrates the point. One of the basic intents of the Charter is to lay down guiding principles governing the relationships between employers and employees and their respective rights and duties towards each other. Many of these principles reflect those that have been proposed and practised as forms of industrial democracy probably since before the emergence of OD itself. Indeed many writers on OD would dispute that industrial democracy is an approach to OD. In my view they would be wrong since, as with other approaches and methodologies, it is not industrial democracy itself which represents OD but how and why it is applied. It also seems to me to be true that there is in any case a close affinity between OD and industrial democracy since they share similar humanistic

values and generally promote the effect of increased organizational learning.

There are many examples of industrial democracy in both theory and practice. The work of Jaques and Brown at Glacier Metal in the UK is one, while in the USA the Scanlon Plan is another famous approach (French, 1984; Handy, 1985; Lee, 1985; Margulies, 1971). Both of these examples suggest specific systems and procedures for ensuring employee participation in decision-making and a share in control over the organization. Such systems and procedures are also designed to develop a different kind of culture based on shared interests and values. While positive results have been reported for the approaches, success cannot be guaranteed. Creating new organizational forms on the basis of the principles of industrial democracy can be a very effective approach to OD and one which can also provide useful methodologies for managing the transitional process.

SOME FURTHER PERSPECTIVES ON OD

The above summary represents the major methodologies developed and applied as part of OD. To conclude this introduction to OD I want to describe some further perspectives on the subject.

The 'excellence' model

The first perspective is provided by what was probably the major book on organization and management published in the 1980s – *In Search of Excellence* (Peters and Waterman 1982). It can be described as the major book of the 1980s because of its phenomenal sales and popularity and, in consequence, its impact on management thinking and practice. Although many of its ideas were not new they were presented in a coherent analysis of what constitutes an 'ideal' organization form. This analysis in turn was based on extensive research into the organizational factors which could be identified as common among the most successful companies in the USA. The experience and performance of some of the 'excellent' organizations after the research and publication of the book provided the basis for criticism of Peters and Waterman's analysis and there were certainly grounds for criticism in the book itself – not least on the research methodology. However, no critical analysis of the book can detract from the major achievement of Peters and Waterman in advancing our understanding of what makes for an effective organization.

In Search of Excellence was not necessarily intended to be, nor need it be seen as, a book on OD. The analysis provided does, however, have two things in common with OD. First, it assumes the existence of an ideal organization form and describes this ideal in some detail. Second, the humanistic values so important in OD are also implicit in the organization form proposed by Peters and Waterman. It is, however, the analytical tool applied by the authors which is most relevant here since it helps to illustrate the nature of OD. This analytical tool is known as the 'Seven Ss' and is represented in diagrammatic form in Figure 4.1.

The organizational factors identified in Figure 4.1, according to Peters and Waterman, need to be mutually supportive and in harmony in order for the organization to be effective. An analysis of each therefore needs to be undertaken and adjustments, or *changes*, made to some or all depending on the results of the analysis, to bring about the necessary supportiveness and harmony. The key factor is that of shared values which was, in the past,

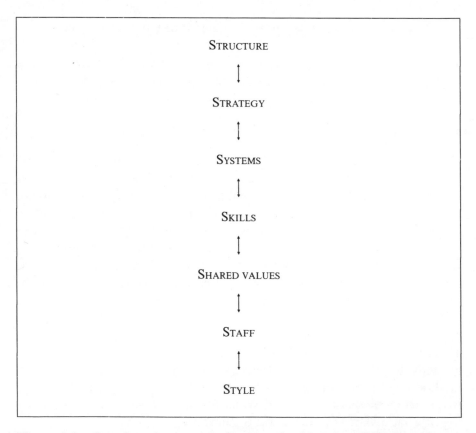

Figure 4.1 *Based on the seven Ss framework of Peters and Waterman* (*Source:* Peters and Waterman, 1982.)

normally not given great attention by senior decision makers in organizations. However, some of the organization factors are easier to deal with, ie, analysis and influence for change, than others. Those that are easiest to deal with can be usefully referred to as 'hard' factors and those which are most difficult as 'soft' factors. There is a certain paradox in these terms since 'hard' equates to easy and 'soft' equates to difficult. Most managers prefer to deal with what is easy and this partly explains why the 'soft' areas of organization life are too often ignored.

We can categorize each of the factors in Figure 4.1 according to whether it is hard or soft. Personally, I prefer all alternative which is a mixture of both with either hard or soft coming first to indicate which is dominant. Using this four-part classification system my analysis of the Peters and Waterman factors is given in the following list:

- Structure   – Hard
- Strategy   – Hard
- Skills   – Hard/Soft
- Systems   – Hard/Soft
- Staff   – Soft/Hard
- Style   – Soft
- Shared values – Soft.

This classification helps to illustrate the meaning of hard and soft. Organization structure and strategy are relatively easy to observe, measure and analyses and, on paper at least, change. Organization style and shared values on the other hand are very difficult to analyse and change (see also Fredericks and Stewart, 1996).

What this analysis of part of the work of Peters and Waterman does is to help illustrate the nature of OD. The focus of attention of OD work is the soft areas of organization life. As an approach to managing change OD is concerned with ensuring that these soft areas are given attention at least equal to that given to the hard areas, and that the soft areas are enabled to provide an engine for change through being utilized for effective organization learning.

The 'Iceberg' model

This essential characteristic is further illustrated in a model of OD proposed in 1978 by Herman (Stoner, 1989; French and Bell, 1990). This model is for me unbeatable in conceiving OD in theory and practice. The analogy is that of an iceberg and Herman's model is given in Figure 4.2.

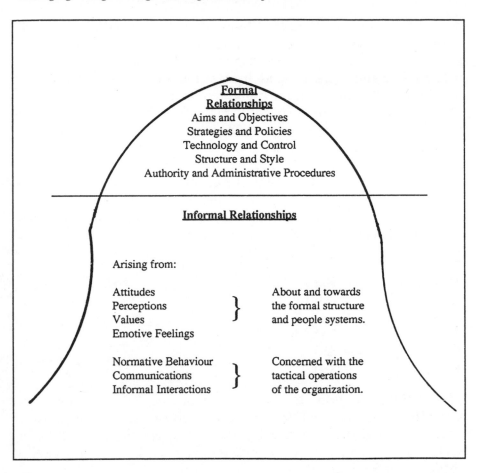

Figure 4.2   *S.N. Herman's 'Iceberg' model of OD (Source:* Stewart, 1994*)*

Figure 4.2 in many ways reflects the discussion of 'hard' and 'soft' areas of organizational life. The hard areas equate to those above the surface; because they are easily visible they are easiest to deal with. The soft areas equate to those below the surface and, therefore, they are more difficult to manage.

Herman's model suggests other truisms of organization life. The bulk of the iceberg is below the surface but forms the stabilizing mass. Unless these soft areas, ie, the informal relationships, truly support the hard areas, the whole of the 'iceberg' or organization will be in danger of collapse. What this means in practice is that it is the informal relationships which are critical to the success or otherwise of the organization. The shifting nature of the informal relationships below the surface also creates forces for change. They are in effect an important internal source of change as discussed in Chapter 2. These forces for change may be functional or dysfunctional, that is they may work towards beneficial or detrimental results for the organization.

Managing change means seeking to ensure beneficial results from such forces for change. Therefore, an essential part of managing change is focusing on the informal relationships, or soft areas, of the organization in order to ensure that the bulk of the experience of organization members leads them to support organizational aims and objectives, strategies and policies. It is in effect the informal rather than the formal relationships in an organization which determine success or failure. The key to success is to ensure a continuing and ongoing 'match' between the two. These arguments are resonant with those advanced to support 'soft' models of HRM (Legge, 1995).

The focus of OD activities is the bulk of the iceberg below the surface. Those informal relationships provide the raw material of OD programmes. It can be argued that the essential purpose of OD is to raise the soft areas of organization life above the surface so that they may be better analysed and managed. Herman's model is certainly useful in illustrating the nature of OD which is to work with the informal relationships to bring about support and harmony between the hard and soft areas of the organization. Such work does not necessarily imply bringing about acceptance of the 'formal' within the 'informal' and often in practice means changing the 'formal' to more closely reflect the 'informal'.

The learning organization

When we have a situation which involves close, regular and constructive interaction between the formal and informal, or hard and soft areas, we have the conditions necessary for effective learning by and within the organization, a fundamental aim of OD. This brings us to a third and final perspective on OD. It is the notion of a 'learning organization'. This concept is considered in detail in Chapter 6.

SUMMARY

We can summarize our discussion of OD so far with one final view of the concept – the 'Gap' model of OD. Its basic idea is represented in Figure 4.3.

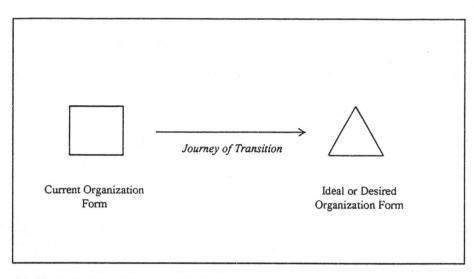

Figure 4.3   *The 'Gap' model of OD*

The 'Gap' model

The geometric shape on the left in Figure 4.3 represents the current organization form. To emphasize the point made earlier, this does not mean the organization structure but the collection of characteristics identified, for example, in Figure 4.1. I could have chosen any shape or other metaphor to represent the organization; there is no significance in choosing a square. The shape on the right of the model represents an ideal or desired organization form. The arrow between the two represents the methods adopted to make the changes required to the present state in order to create the future state. OD is an approach to managing that process of change.

However, implicit in OD are at least two characteristics which need to be incorporated in the ideal form on the right of the model. These are an increased ability to learn and change, and the adoption of humanistic values in the organization and management style. Also, OD implies certain prescriptions about processes to use to both manage the change or transition, represented by the arrow, and to reach decisions on other aspects of the ideal organization form. These prescriptions are implicit in and are derived from the three sets of assumptions described earlier in the chapter. It is the meeting of these prescriptions on ideal form, change processes and decision making which determine whether or not OD is being practised in a particular set of activities.

A criticism of OD

It would be unwise to leave this chapter without acknowledging the criticisms which have been made of the theory and practice of OD. Much of the criticism rests on disagreement with the prescriptions inherent in OD. This is particularly true of the emphasis on humanistic values in OD, closely identified with the parallel development of the Human Relations school of management largely founded by Mayo and his colleagues (French 1984; Wilson 1990). The major criticism is founded on the belief that humanistic values fail to take account of the realities of, for example, market influences in determining organization success, and that they inhibit the incorporation of theories to do with power in its many forms within organizations (Legge, 1995). For example, any strictly capitalist or Marxist economic analysis of organisation and management would discount the validity and value of OD. I acknowledge the existence and possible validity of such criticisms. However, any objective assessment of research would reveal contradictory and competing evidence. With a lack of conclusive evidence in either direction, ie, proving or disproving the value of OD, we are left with forming personal judgements. My own judgement based on personal experience is that OD is not only an effective tool in managing change but an essential one for HRM and training practitioners.

5. Three major OD methodologies

Organization development represents a particular philosophy of managing organization change which takes its theory and practice from the social sciences. My summary of its history and progress in the previous chapter illustrated the many themes and approaches considered appropriate and effective. The examination and analysis of the philosophy also indicated some of the critical features of OD which distinguish it from other approaches to organization change. This chapter will add further illumination to those features by describing three particular methodologies developed by leading OD theorists. The methodologies chosen are all long-established in the practice of OD. They are particularly significant and interesting for three reasons. First, while they are not new they are still widely practised within organizations throughout the world and, in my view, are still as relevant today as when they were first devised. Second, they have between them formed the basis of most of the more recently developed methods, tools and techniques of OD. While it may have been unconscious to those who devised them, it is difficult to identify many new and current techniques which cannot be related theoretically to the three methodologies described in this chapter. Finally, they are very helpful in illustrating what is OD and what is not by showing how the principles are applied in practice. This is because the theorists who devised the methodologies were at the forefront of developing OD as a discrete organization discipline. The following chapter on the learning organization explores the most recent conceptualization of OD and ends our examination of change at organization level.

The three methodologies examined in the chapter are The Leadership Grid, Survey Feedback Method and Process Consultation. I want first though to make an important point which applies to them all. This is simply that they do not have to be used and applied as described here. There are many ways of adapting the principles and techniques for different purposes and contexts. Equally their use is not mutually exclusive and so they can be used in combination. Indeed, it can be argued with great justification that the third methodology, Process Consultation, is an integral and essential ingredient of all OD programmes. So, while I describe the methodologies with as much accuracy and faith to the originators as I can achieve, you should not be inhibited from devising your own methods or techniques within the general frameworks offered. Doing so is an everyday activity for OD and training practitioners alike since, like managing itself, OD is neither science nor art but a *pragmatic* combination of both. To finalize the point, it is entirely possible that many readers are already using variants of the methodologies, as indicated in the last chapter in relation to the Managerial Grid, perhaps without even knowing it!

THE LEADERSHIP GRID®

Blake and Mouton have been expounding the effectiveness of their Managerial Grid for over 30 years (Blake and Mouton, 1964, 1978, 1985). (The most recent text concerning this theory is *Leadership Dilemmas – Grid Solutions* (Blake and McCanse, 1991) and the Grid Figure is now labelled the 'Leadership Grid'.) Given that time-scale there is an abundance of research evidence available on the efficacy of this particular method. The problem is that the evidence is contradictory and therefore inconclusive. While many studies have been done on the effects of Managerial Grid OD programmes it sometimes seems to be the case that those that find beneficial outcomes are equalled numerically at least by those which find either no benefit or detrimental results. This situation is easily explained by the problems of conducting research in the area of organization behaviour. An obvious problem is that of time-scale, since most Managerial Grid-based OD programmes last a minimum of 18 months and probably average three years in length. Given such time-scales for the programme, when is it appropriate to expect to observe results? These time-scales compound a second problem, that of isolating cause and effect. While changes may be observed, detrimental or beneficial, it is certainly impossible to hold other factors constant and therefore probably impossible to conclusively attribute any change purely to the OD programme. Even studies which are based on the research model of 'control groups', ie, comparing performance over time of organizations which have been subject to Managerial Grid programmes with similar organizations operating in similar environments which have not, cannot really claim to have isolated and accounted for all other intervening variables. A third problem is that of measurement in what is, as we shall see, the major focus of Managerial Grid programmes, ie, management style. Most if not all means of measurement in this area rely on 'reported information' based either on self-analysis or analysis by others.

There are whole libraries of books on research methodology covering this problem.

What is certainly the case is that the originators of the method have never lost faith in their creation; neither have hundreds of practitioners and perhaps hundreds of thousands of satisfied clients. Blake and Mouton themselves have published many books over the last 30 years defending the principles of Managerial Grid and revising its operation in OD in response to newly emerging theories and, perhaps, if we were to be unkind, new fashions. My own judgement is that the Managerial Grid has much to commend it and that it provides many useful ideas for applying OD in practice. But, what exactly is the method?

The nature of the Leadership Grid

Essentially, the Leadership Grid rests on a number of very simple propositions. The first is that all organizations have three features in common. These usefully abbreviate to the 'Three Ps': Purpose, People and Power. The first two are fairly obvious and self-explanatory. All organizations, irrespective of size or economic sector, come into being and seek to survive in order to serve some purpose from which their goals and objectives are derived. In organization and management theory this is now usually referred to as the 'organization mission'. That organizations all share the characteristic of 'people' is inherent in the definition of the word with the possible exception of owner/manager businesses. The third 'P' is more interesting. Everyone's personal experience testifies to the existence of power in organizations. It is normally also true that power is unevenly or unequally distributed and that it derives from a number of different sources (Johnson, 1996). The traditional method of providing a source of power and controlling its distribution is through a hierarchical structure. It is well understood in management theory that there are many other sources or forms of power, eg, positional, sapiential, charismatic, and that it is to misunderstand the concept to think of power in finite terms. It can be created and added to within organizations. However, it is true of most if not all organizations that the most significant and effective power is that vested in hierarchical status and it is this source of power which is referred to in the 'Three Ps'.

The second proposition underpinning the Leadership Grid is that the most significant variable determining organization effectiveness is the way power is exercised. In simple terms, what matters most in organizations is how power is exercised over people in the pursuit of purpose, and that achievement of purpose is dependent upon how power is exercised over people. This is undoubtedly a gross oversimplification of Blake and Mouton's work but it represents the essential argument. Obviously it is accepted that many other factors influence and determine organization success, some of them outside the control of the organization. But, according to the Leadership Grid, the most important is the exercise of power by those in 'powerful' positions. The manifestation and operation of

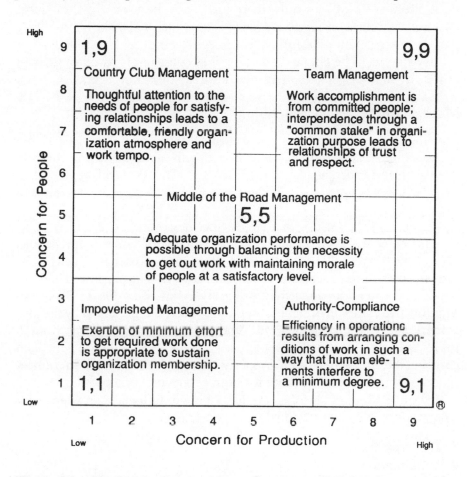

Figure 5.1 *The Leadership Grid Figure® (Source:* Blake and McCanse, 1991*)*

(The Leadership Grid® Figure from *Leadership Dilemmas – Grid Solutions*, by Robert R. Blake and Anne Adams McCanse. Houston: Gulf Publishing Co., p. 29. Copyright © 1991, by Scientific Methods Inc. Reproduced by permission of the owners.)

this power is through 'management style'. Individual managers exercise their power over their subordinates in different ways according to their individual assumptions about factors such as work, themselves, people in general and their subordinates in particular. This leads to the idea that management style is critical in determining organization effectiveness.

There are two final propositions. The first is that while a range of styles are possible there exists variability in effectiveness and that one style will be the most effective. In other words, there exists one 'best' or 'right' or 'most effective' way of exercising power over people which will make it most likely that the organization will continually achieve its purpose. The second is that this style needs to be adopted and exercised consistently by all those with power, ie, all managers, in order to achieve organization success.

Management style and leadership

Building on these propositions and drawing on their own research and that of others into leadership behaviour and effectiveness, Blake and Mouton devised their Leadership Grid approach to OD. The Grid, represents a range of styles adopted by individual managers, and these are described in Figure 5.1.

The basis of the Grid is that two factors determine management style: amount of concern for production *and* amount of concern for people. Management style will in turn determine how power is exercised which in its turn will determine organization success in achieving its purpose. There are within the Grid a wide range of possible styles but, according to Blake and Mouton, five common or significant ones. These are represented by the four corners and the centre of the Grid. Again according to Blake and Mouton the required style for effective use of power is that located in the top right hand corner of the Grid. This is known as a 9,9 orientation, or Team Management style which reflects high concern for both production and people.

Blake and Mouton identify a number of major influences on which style will be adopted by an individual manager. These are:

- The Organization
- The Situation
- Personal Values
- Personality
- Chance.

The first of these recognizes that the organization itself influences the behaviour of its individual members, including managers. At a basic level this means that an individual manager may have an established management style represented by, say, a 1,9 orientation on taking up a new job in a new organization. Over a period of time this style may be influenced in an alternative direction, say, towards a 9,1 orientation, and therefore the individual's established management style becomes less dominant in determining behaviour in favour of the alternative. The alternative may in fact take over as a new established management style for the individual manager. Various characteristics of the organization will influence the adoption of management style. The critical 'cluster' of characteristics which will be most significant are those which are now referred to collectively as 'organization culture'. As the culture of an organization is both an input and an output in relation to behaviour; that is, it is both a consequence of and cause of the behaviour of organization members, it is obviously a significant factor in influencing the management style adopted by individual members.

The second factor in the list arises out of and in response to research and theory which argues a contingency approach to leadership behaviour. The basic argument is that there is no one best management style; rather which style will be most effective is determined by situational variables. The propositions described earlier as underpinning the Leadership Grid clearly demonstrate that Blake and Mouton reject this argument. They do, however, accept that situational factors will influence what style is adopted and that an individual manager may therefore behave differently in differing circumstances. This is not the same as different organizations. It is to do with the fluidity of organization life in relation to changing tasks, pressures and personalities. Blake and Mouton concede that such factors will influence the expression of management style to some extent through a range of behaviours but argue that this does not negate the existence of a dominant or preferred style. Nor does it negate the greater effectiveness of a 9,9 orientation in all circumstances. The argument largely rests on the next two influencing factors.

Individual values and personality are seen as being the most significant influences on management style and therefore leadership behaviour. This is because those behaviours are based on the dominant assumptions held by the individual about what is 'good' or 'bad', 'right' or 'wrong', 'effective' or 'ineffective'. These assumptions are reflected in and expressed by the individual's values and personality which in turn shape behaviour. However, within the theory which underpins the Leadership Grid such assumptions are the result of learning through experience and therefore can be challenged and changed. This does not imply a total personality change but it does mean that individuals can and do adopt different value systems if the basis of their dominant assumptions is altered. Altering the assumptions of individual managers is a central focus of OD through the Leadership Grid.

The final influencing factor in the list is that of chance. The operation of chance is acknowledged in science as a phenomenon acting in accordance with as yet unknown laws, perhaps explicable only through 'chaos theory', and is accepted by Blake and Mouton as potentially significant. In terms of management style, chance may play a part in shaping the operation of the other influencing factors, eg, bringing about congruence or incongruence, in relation to specific acts by the manager arising from particular circumstances. It is not seen as a factor which is very significant in terms of determining general or ongoing management style.

The Managerial Grid OD programme

Having identified these influencing factors Blake and Mouton go on to argue that to produce the most effective management style requires all of the factors to be aligned in the direction of that style. That is, that there must be congruence between all of the factors in their influence on each individual manager's dominant style. Achieving that congruence is the major aim of a Grid OD programme. Once that is achieved, the organization will be effective in OD terms and therefore will be in a position to maximize its effectiveness in terms of its own objectives and preferred performance measures.

A Managerial Grid OD programme itself consists of six stages:

Stage 1 – Grid Seminars
Stage 2 – Team Building
Stage 3 – Intergroup Development
Stage 4 – Ideal Strategic Model
Stage 5 – Implementation
Stage 6 – Consolidation.

1. Grid Seminars
The first stage, Grid Seminars, have an individual focus in the sense that they are aimed at individual managers. However, since all managers throughout the organization are normally expected to attend they also have an organization focus. The purpose of the seminars is to train managers in the concepts and operation of the Grid and to enable them to learn new management styles. Out of this training comes a commonly held and applied

9,9 management style. The design of the Seminars has its roots in the NTL 'T' Groups although in recent years they have come to have a very structured methodology (see Chapter 11). Application of the Grid Seminars has the effect of ensuring the influencing factors of values and personality support a 9.9 orientation and begins the process of achieving congruence between those and the influencing factor of organization culture.

2. Team Building

Team Building, as the term implies, is a set of activities aimed at intact and discrete work teams in the organization. After attending a Grid Seminar individual managers experience Stage 2 with their direct subordinates. This stage again is intended to encompass the whole of the organization so that all organization members are involved. The purpose is to increase the effectiveness of work teams in terms of their problem solving ability. This is achieved through examining and improving how the team works together. It also has the effect of reinforcing the 9,9 Team Manager orientation of the individual manager. Since the stage is again applied throughout the organization it has the additional effect of producing common ways of working.

3. Intergroup Development

The second effect is further reinforced and extended through the third stage, Intergroup Development. The focus here is multiple groupings in the organization such as teams from marketing and production. The aim is to examine and improve the way different functions, departments or sections work together in support of achieving organization objectives. Issues considered in this stage will include items such as systems for coordination and communication, attitudes towards different functions, and interpersonal relationships between individuals in different departments. There are many possibilities in terms of design of activities in this stage.

4. Ideal Strategic Model

Stage 4 concerns only the top management team of the organization. It may be appropriate at this point to say a word about timing and organization. The six stages of Grid OD are sequential and must occur in the order listed. However, depending on the size of the organization, stages can run concurrently. If the organization is large then once a critical mass of individual managers have experienced seminars, Stage 2 can commence. Similarly with Stages 2 and 3. Once a number of teams have experienced team building then intergroup development can begin. Defining the 'organization' at the start of a Grid OD programme is critical for the operation of these stages. It does not have to be the whole entity but can be a division or branch or department within a total organization. Once the preceding stages are nearing completion throughout the defined organization, Stage 4 can be undertaken.

The purpose of this stage is to enable top management to work on defining their ideal organization and to devise a strategy for achieving it. The output then is an organization strategy for a given time period, usually long-term. Locating this activity at this stage in an OD programme is sometimes questioned since other approaches would put the activity at the beginning of a change programme. Many writers on organizations and management argue that strategy formulation is an essential starting point. However, such arguments are outside the tradition of OD as defined in this book. The OD argument is that the organization first needs to be an effective learning system before any strategy can work in practice, and that all of the characteristics of the organization – the soft as well as the hard areas – need to be mutually supportive of achieving the strategy. The earlier stages of a Managerial Grid OD programme are intended to create those conditions.

5. Implementation and 6. Consolidation
The final two stages of a Grid programme follow sequentially and logically from Stage 4. They are to do with implementing the strategy throughout the organization and moving it towards the ideal model. As part of this, arrangements need to be designed and applied for monitoring and evaluating results. This leads to consolidation of the benefits of the total programme. A total Grid OD programme, depending on the size of the organization, is likely to take a minimum of three years, so such programmes are difficult to assess in terms of their efficacy.

The Leadership Grid and OD

The Grid approach to OD illustrates the major principles of the discipline. First, in its focus on the team manager management style, which is based on a high concern for people as well as production, it incorporates the humanistic values inherent in OD. A second application of this principle is in the operation of the stages of the programme. The second and third stages involve all organization members in working on improvements in organization functioning. This implies complete involvement in decision making on issues which directly affect their experience of the organization. Methods adopted in Stages 5 and 6 also reflect similar principles. A Grid programme also explicitly adopts the idea of an 'ideal' organization model, and it contains two prescriptions on the nature of this model for all organizations. The first is effective learning through improved working and relationships within and between teams; the second is in terms of dominant management style. Both of these promote a particular form of organization culture.

Leadership Grid applications

A total and integrated Grid OD programme implies a significant investment of time, effort and expense. It also requires the services of a trained and licensed practitioner. Such a person will have access to all of the supporting materials and expertise from Blake's consultancy corporation. However, many of the principles of Grid OD can and have been applied outside of a total programme by a wide range of people.

Many management development programmes have as their rationale a focus on producing a consistent and congruent management style throughout the organization. Often, such a style reflects the principles of the grid 9.9 orientation although this may not be explicit. Many of the training or learning methodologies utilized in these programmes have their origins in those devised for use in grid seminars. So, it can be argued that organizations all over the world are practising elements of Grid OD. The practitioners involved are of course mostly internal training and development practitioners.

All of the preceding points also apply to team building. The purpose and methods commonly utilized owe a great debt to Blake and Mouton. Stage 3 of the Grid programme is a major approach to OD which is commonly practised. Many techniques in OD such as confrontation meetings or organizational mirroring are designed and used to aid intergroup development. Finally, strategy development workshops are an increasingly popular method of managing organization change. Such an approach usually involves the top management team working with the help of an external or internal consultant in the role of facilitator. This is exactly what happens in Stage 4 of a Grid programme.

So we can see that specialist practitioners and a total programme are not necessarily required to apply Grid OD in practice. Blake and Mouton and their followers may argue that variants or part programmes are unlikely to achieve success. My own judgement is that this is not the case. It is useful, perhaps essential, though, in my view, for HRM and training and development practitioners to know and understand the theoretical base of their decisions and actions.

THE SURVEY FEEDBACK METHOD IN OD

The second major methodology in OD I wish to examine in this chapter is that of Survey Feedback.

The basic principles of Survey Feedback were first coherently expounded by Beckhard (Bennis, 1969; French, 1984; Margulies, 1971). As the term implies, the method consists of two separate stages: data collection followed by examination and discussion of the results. This fact distinguishes the method from activities such as attitude surveys which may appear similar. Survey Feedback means all of those involved in providing data in the first stage are also involved in the second stage. For this reason it is critical that those ultimately responsible for dealing with and resolving the issues and problems identified are committed to doing so, and practitioners must ensure that they have a clear and appropriate contract agreed with decision makers before using the method.

When to use the method

This last point perhaps leads to the question of when Survey Feedback is an appropriate method. Some useful indicators are:

- When there is evidence of *subordinate dissatisfaction* with *management* approach and style.
- *Decision* making is *poor*, eg, centralized and autocratic, with little delegation.
- *Crisis* management or *fire-fighting* appear to be the norm.
- *Goals* and objectives are *unclear*.
- *Roles* and responsibilities are *confused*.
- *Morale* is low, perhaps related to *major change* taking place.

This list is not intended to be definitive or exhaustive. The items on it are also not likely to occur in isolation or independently. Major change may cause confusion over roles and responsibilities and consequently low morale, or autocratic decision making may be a feature of management style which causes subordinate dissatisfaction. It is probably the case too that the list contains features which are likely to be true of all organizations at some time in their history. Survey Feedback is not a universal panacea appropriate in all circumstances, but it is capable of wide application.

Purpose and operation of the method

The major purpose of the method is to enable managers, boss and subordinates or other work groups to collaborate in identifying and working to improve deficiencies in organizational effectiveness. A second though no less important purpose is to enable such groups to improve their individual and collective ability to solve common problems. In this sense, Survey Feedback is a means of developing the *process* skills of those taking part in order to provide a sounder future ability in managing organization change. Precise details and techniques of the method will depend on whether it is being applied throughout a total organization, within one department or division, with a management team only, or with one particular work group. The general principles described in the following paragraphs will apply in all cases.

The data collection stage usually involves some form of written 'instrument'. It may be a highly structured questionnaire or be very open in participant responses. Many commercially available, standard instruments can be used or the practitioner can produce original formats to suit particular circumstances. Whatever decisions are reached two important principles need to be observed in this stage. The first is that the focus of the instrument is respondents' perceptions of, feelings about and attitudes towards the organizational issue of concern, eg, management style or roles and responsibilities. In other words, the focus is the bulk of the iceberg in Herman's model of OD given in Figure 4.2. The second principle is that all members of the group using the method are included in the survey and provide information about themselves. This means, for instance, if the group is an individual manager and work team then the manager completes the instrument and the responses of all concern that team rather than the organization as a whole.

Some factors commonly examined in using the Survey Feedback method and therefore forming the focus of data collection include the following:

- Perceptions of performance criteria and achievement.
- Clarity of goals and objectives.
- Organization structure.
- Management information and control systems.
- Personal relationships.
- Management style.
- Effectiveness of communications.
- Decision making procedures.
- Conduct of meetings.

There are a number of possible outcomes to the survey. First, it may confirm the group's existing collective perception. Second, it may contradict existing perceptions. Both of these are possible and sometimes occur but they are less likely than the final two possibilities. The third is that differing perceptions are identified among group members. A variant of this is the fourth possibility of common perceptions being held by identifiable sub-groups different to those held by other sub-groups, eg, all managers have a shared perception of decision making while all subordinates have a different shared perception.

These latter two possible outcomes are very common and potentially much more productive. Examining reasons for the results can often identify and bring to the surface issues not directly related to the data themselves. Such issues can often be even more dysfunctional and their resolution therefore can lead to more effective functioning in the future.

A major strength of the Survey Feedback method is that the data generated belong to and are 'owned' by the organizational members involved. They are not given or provided by some external agency; it is not a consultant saying the organization or group has this or that weakness but the members themselves. It is critical therefore that this ownership continues during the Feedback stage.

Feedback normally occurs at a meeting or series of meetings of the group surveyed and/or relevant sub-groups. Individual data are shared and collated at these meetings although, if large numbers are involved, the OD practitioner may produce collated results prior to the meeting(s). The purpose of the meetings is to analyse and interpret the data, identify consequences and agree future action for dealing with the results. Action agreed is likely to include immediate, short-term and long-term plans, and will continue to involve all group members. The group itself is responsible for the conduct of the feedback meeting(s) and managing agreed action. The role of the OD practitioner is to help and facilitate those processes.

Group interaction at Feedback meetings helps to clarify and bring into the open individual positions, clarify and establish group norms and to develop more effective working relationships. In a sense these outcomes are a secondary agenda of the method which is primarily addressed during the Feedback stage. Pursuit of these objectives provides a real opportunity for the OD practitioner to be of benefit to the group in helping them become aware of their own process issues. In doing this, the aim is to enable the group to become efficient in monitoring and improving its own process. Once achieved, it is likely that the group will develop norms of behaviour and patterns of working which support productive work through problem solving and a change orientation.

It will be clear from this description that Survey Feedback, in common with the Leadership Grid, incorporates the 'ideal' organization form model and humanistic values of OD. The method enables all group members to be involved in identifying characteristics which need to be changed and in implementing actions to improve effectiveness. It will also be clear that the role and skills required of the OD practitioner using the method mean that training and HRM professionals are ideally suited to offer such a service. So long as the principles are adhered to, it is a very simple method for them to adopt on the basis of their own designs and materials.

Survey Feedback applications

Organization Blockage approach
A well established and useful approach to OD which reflects the principles of the Survey Feedback method is the 'Organization Blockage', a design devised by Woodcock and Francis (Woodcock and Francis, 1979). The basis of this method is a 120-item instrument which examines 12 critical issues which can block organization effectiveness. The items are clear statements about the issue which respondents have to decide are either true or false of their organization. Collation of individual results is quick and simple through a summary grid which scores the results under 12 columns representing the 12 issues. The use of this method is through six simple stages:

1. Define the organization.
2. Define target audience (ideally, all members of Stage 1).
3. Target audience complete instrument individually.
4. Target audience meet to share and examine results.
5. Group agree priorities for attention (between 2 and 4 from 12 issues).
6. Group discuss and agree action.

Woodcock and Francis have published a wide range of materials to help and support examination of and action on each of the 12 potential blockages. However, though they are useful they are not essential and groups can devise their own approaches and materials with the help of an OD practitioner. Similarly, practitioners can very easily design and use their own instruments following the model suggested by the originators.

Problem Identification Meetings
A second example of the Survey Feedback method was originally designed as an approach to the training and development of supervisors, adopting an

OD methodology as an alternative to the previously dominant common skills approach. It is a method called Problem Identification Meetings (PIMs), the operation of one of which is described in Figure 5.2. The description clearly demonstrates the nature of the Survey Feedback method and its ease of adaptation and use.

Stage One - Pre-Work

Supervisors are asked to respond to the following questions.

(i) Please identify what you believe to be the 5 main responsibilities of your job and what proportion of your time you spend on each.

(ii) What are the 5 main difficulties you face in doing your job?

(iii) Please list 5 actions that you think should be taken to help make your job easier and your performance more effective. Include any ideas on training and development that you think may help.

Stage Two - The Meeting

The meeting is opened, chaired and led by a Senior Manager with other managers attending. The trainer facilitates the process. This consists of the supervisors working in syndicates to complete Group Tasks on reaching consensus based on their individual responses in the pre-work. Each syndicate also produces and presents a report on their conclusions in plenary session. This leads to a discussion to reach agreement on priorities and future action. Action is likely to involve the senior manager, other managers and the supervisors themselves. It may also include provision of training and development activities. Dates are set for future meetings and the senior manager closes the meeting.

Stage Three - Ongoing Action

Agreed action is implemented, monitored and reviewed. This ongoing process continues so long as required by the organization.

Figure 5.2 *Problem identification meeting*

An 'Excellence' based method
The final example of application is derived from the Peters and Waterman (1982) book *In Search of Excellence*. It simply provides a summary on one sheet of paper of the characteristics of the excellent organization. A second sheet then asks respondents to rate their organization, however defined, against those characteristics and to provide reasons supported by examples for their rating. When utilized through the six stages identified for the organizational blockage approach of Woodcock and Francis, the instrument is simply an alternative focus for what is essentially the same method of Survey Feedback.

An important principle
It is perhaps important to emphasize a feature of Survey Feedback which is implicit in all three examples: that the feedback is simply that. There is no assessment or judgemental evaluation of the data. The resulting data are fed back to organization or group members exactly as they emerge. The practitioner is simply using the method to hold up a mirror to the organization. It is for the organization to make sense of and evaluate the reflection. This feature of the Survey Feedback method is also in some ways present in the final major method within OD, described below.

PROCESS CONSULTATION

Before examining Process Consultation (PC) in detail it will be helpful to reinforce the point made earlier that the methods described in this chapter are not mutually exclusive either with themselves or other alternative approaches. This is particularly true of PC. While it can and often does form the principle methodology adopted in an OD programme it is also probably the case that *all* OD programmes include at some point a need for PC. Practitioners therefore need a sound understanding of and ability to practise PC. Why this is the case will become clear in this section.

Process Consultation described

My description of PC assumes that it is being utilized as the major methodology in an OD programme. As a starting point it is useful to contrast PC with other forms of consultancy. Two common ones are those of Doctor–Patient and Lawyer–Client. In both of these cases there are two significant features which characterize the relationship. First, the person being consulted is an *expert* who is expected to provide *solutions*. Second, and following from this, there is a high degree of *dependency* on the part of the client, that is, the client needs the expert to provide guidance on action and usually accepts the advice given. It could be argued that there is a third significant feature in these relationships which is that neither expert (doctor or lawyer) nor client (patient or litigant) wants or expects that dependency to diminish for the duration of the consultancy assignment. The end of the assignment will be reached with the success or failure of the expert-provided solution. Similar relationships exist in organization consultancy. Assignments are often undertaken by subject or technical consultants, for example in marketing, advertising, production or finance, which are characterized by expert-provided solutions to a dependent client. PC in contrast is not about providing expert advice or solutions. Rather, it is about helping clients to develop the ability to diagnose and solve their own problems. The 'client' in this sense can be an organization, a work group, a team or an individual. In each case however, given that organizations are living systems, the client is likely to be part of a wider entity and therefore it is usual to think in terms of a 'client system'.

PC then is concerned with developing ability in the client system and thereby decreasing dependency on the consultant. This will necessarily involve the clients in a learning process and therefore require them to decide on their own actions. For this reason a process consultant is unlikely to provide solutions. All of these points are well summarized in the definition of PC first offered by Schein (1969):

A set of activities on the part of the consultant which help the client to perceive, understand and act upon process events which occur in the client's environment.

PC assumptions

The definition rests on a rationale which contains some implicit assumptions. These assumptions are made explicit and explained in the following list:

- Managers in work organizations do not always know what is wrong or problematic and therefore what kind of help they need.
- Organizations are capable of being more effective and generally have a constructive intent to improve.
- External consultants cannot know or understand the organization culture and what will be appropriate and therefore must work with those that do.

- Responsibility for action and decision making rests and must remain with the clients. They have to live with the consequences.
- The role of the Process Consultant is to pass on effective diagnostic and process skills to the client.

The last point in the list emphasizes that the consultant has a training and development role, ie, in developing the skill of the client. This is normally achieved through acting as a facilitator rather than as a direct trainer but it does illustrate a sound rationale for HRM and HRD specialists providing PC within organizations. Even where such specialists are employed by the organization, the point concerning 'external' consultants can often still apply depending on the size of the organization. Experience and research indicates that HRM/HRD specialists do in fact often act as Process Consultants to their organizations and that this is sometimes characterized by what is known as the 'change agent' role of training professionals.

PC in practice

In looking at what is actually involved in PC in practice, the first step is to define 'process'. It is simply one of the human processes within organizations. An indicative list of such processes is:

- Communications.
- Decision Making.
- Problem Solving.
- Intergroup Cooperation.
- Leadership.
- Interpersonal Relationships.

Items such as those in the list provide the focus for PC. This is not to discount the importance of other functions and processes within organizations such as production, marketing or accounting. Each function will have its own technical processes which are of course critical in determining organizational effectiveness. It also may be worth recording here that PC does not imply any criticism of other forms of consultancy such as the expert provider of solutions. That may be wholly appropriate when dealing with technical processes. However, it is important to realize that the human processes in an organization link and mediate all other functions and processes, and that all other functions and processes are dependent upon the human processes for their effectiveness. The technical processes in, for example, production cannot work to their best without sound leadership and interpersonal relationships. The various contributions of, say, accounting and sales similarly cannot be effectively coordinated without clear communication and decision making.

It should be clear that individuals acting as Process Consultants need a sound understanding of the psychological and sociological theories which seek to explain and understand these human processes. They also need to be skilled in process observation and analysis (a subject returned to later in the book). The point again provides evidence of the appropriateness of HRM/HRD specialists providing PC services. There is no other organization function where such expertise can realistically be expected to reside.

Given the focus of human processes, the activities of PC generally fall under two headings: diagnosis and intervention. This broad distinction is however more useful as a theoretical framework and guide to action than a description of reality, because diagnosis is itself a form of intervention in the client system, and any intervention will generate new data and so lead to further diagnosis. Thus, while diagnosis is primarily concerned with data gathering, and intervention primarily concerned with effecting change, each set of activities will inform and have consequences for the other.

Within the general headings of Diagnosis and Intervention most PC programmes consist of a number of identifiable stages. Schein proposes the following list:

- *Establishing Contact*
  This first stage occurs when client and consultant first come together to discuss a possible project. Initiating a project can arise for a variety of reasons but usually involves a manager experiencing a felt need or problem. The main focus of the stage is defining and agreeing both a formal and psychological contract. The former is to do with practical items such as time-scales, commitment of consultant days, costs, etc. The latter is about roles, expectations, contributions.

- *Selecting Setting and Method*
  This stage is concerned with agreeing the focus of the work, eg, individual manager, management team, work group, whole department; and methodology, eg, single or group interviews, observation. The major application of method agreed as part of this stage is for diagnosis.

- *Data Gathering*
  Application of the agreed diagnostic method is the focus of this stage in

order to collect and analyse data. This should of course actively involve those in the client system, defined as setting, and not merely the consultant.

● *Intervention*
The data gathering stage will have the effect of increasing the client system's ability to diagnose process problems through their active involvement. This stage, however, is primarily concerned with action by the consultant. The purpose will be to effect change in the processes of the client system and, through that, bring about improved ability on the part of the client system to manage process issues. There are a range of possibilities such as agenda setting workshops, problem identification sessions, coaching, team building activities, suggestions on structure or systems, and individual counselling.

● *Evaluation*
As the term implies, this stage is concerned with measuring benefits. Because of the nature of PC the focus is the client or client system and changes in terms of values and skills in managing human processes.

● *Disengagement*
This final stage occurs naturally out of the preceding one. As the client's ability develops, dependence on and involvement of the consultant reduces. It is often a difficult stage to recognize and manage.

The overall purpose and primary activity of PC is helping groups of people in work organizations manage their ways of interacting more effectively. For this reason, a particular focus of psychological theory of interest is that concerning the dynamics of groups. The application includes PC but also has wider relevance to managing change since it is often the work group represented by a particular department, division or section which is the focus of change. Bringing about change within the dynamics of a group of people is also central to the work of training practitioners. These issues are examined in Chapter 7.

CASE STUDY 2: OD IN PRACTICE – THE FINANCE DEPARTMENT

Within a large commercial organization the HQ corporate Finance Department provided services to operating divisions. Traditionally many of the 'services' were in fact part of the central corporate financial control systems and the operating divisions had no choice about using them. Indeed, the divisions resented not being free to buy in such services from other providers since they felt the charges levied on them to finance the services were not reasonable. Operating divisions also resented the power the corporate department wielded over them in applying the services. For example, one service provided was a computerized payroll which the Finance Department used to ensure that divisions stayed within agreed staffing budgets.

For a variety of reasons the Corporate Board decided to relax some of their controls on operating divisions including allowing them to buy certain financial services from any supplier. This had obvious implications for the Finance Department and in particular one section responsible for the now-relaxed services: it would only survive so long as its services were bought. Three problems were evident. First, the pricing of the section's services had to be competitive. Second, its services had to be truly services and not control systems, ie, they had to meet the needs of the operating divisions and not the control functions of a corporate Finance Department. Third, the traditionally cool relationships between the section and divisions had to become warmer. All of these problems were even more critical since increasing competitiveness and other changes in the organization's market place were impacting on the operating divisions and sharpening further their critical appraisal of the cost and quality of their suppliers.

The corporate Director responsible for the Finance Department asked my help. Together with the Assistant Director responsible for the section directly affected we agreed a three-stage strategy. First, it seemed important to ensure that staff in the section understood all of the factors affecting their future in order to involve them in designing solutions; a series of Information Days was therefore organized. These in fact lasted only half a day but were extremely constructive. Senior managers from all of the operating divisions attended the sessions to describe their operations, problems and requirements of financial services. The sessions were chaired by the Assistant Director (Finance) and following the presentations from operating divisions, staff discussed the implications for their section.

Second, a form of Survey Feedback was utilized to involve all staff in managing required changes. This was a variant of the Problem Identification Meeting. All staff attended a series of full-day sessions chaired by the Finance Director and which I facilitated with the Assistant Director. Staff completed pre-work, which is shown in Figure 5.3. These meetings produced agreement on immediate priorities to be tackled by staff within the section and the Finance Director himself. This led to the formation of four project groups, as the third stage in the strategy, to work on producing recommendations on changes required within the section to meet the future challenges. These project groups drew membership from all levels in the section and their work was coordinated by a Steering Committee chaired by the Head of the section. Once the project groups had begun their work my involvement ceased but I know that in the first year the section won contracts with all operating divisions.

Question 1.	What are the main changes affecting your organization over the next few years?
Question 2.	How will these changes affect the work of your section?
Question 3.	How should your section change the way it does its work as a consequence of the changes?
Question 4.	What do you and your colleagues need to do to make these changes happen?
Question 5.	What do other staff in the Finance Department need to do to make the changes happen?
Question 6.	What other things, if any, would you like to see happen to help your section in the future?

Figure 5.3 *Pre-work for corporate Finance Department staff*

CASE STUDY 3: OD IN PRACTICE – THE DEPARTMENTAL MANAGEMENT TEAM

The core of the Departmental Management Team had been together for a number of years although one person had recently been promoted to a higher position within the team, ie, to Deputy Departmental Head and her place taken by an internal promotee. The Departmental Head and the rest of the established members began to feel that they were in something of a rut and were not working together as well as they should. The catalyst for bringing these feelings to the surface was the new member. There were, however, no particular operational problems that anyone could identify and the performance of the Department was satisfactory on all key measures.

Having been requested by the Department Head to provide some help, I suggested that I should attend a scheduled meeting of the team with my presence and possible involvement in some activity as the final agenda item. This was agreed. I merely observed the meeting until the agenda item and then asked the team to discuss what it was they wanted or expected of me. From my observation of the meeting to that point and the ensuing discussion it seemed obvious that the longer-serving team members had evolved norms of behaviour within their meetings which were not acceptable to the new member. Through a limited number of contributions from me in the form of questions the team members themselves came to the same diagnosis. Having helped the team to that conclusion I then suggested they discuss what could or should be done about the problem. Continuing to observe the discussion it seemed to me that all members of the team were skilled in managing process issues and that there really was no further role for me after the meeting finished. The end of the discussion on what to do about the problem, in which I played no part, was a commitment from each team member to devote the next scheduled meeting to examining current norms and to prepare individually by thinking about strengths and weaknesses. I was then invited by the Department Head to attend that meeting. I asked the question why of the whole team and agreed with their answer that I was not really required.

This example illustrates PC in action. My attendance at the meeting was primarily for diagnostic reasons, as were some of the questions I posed. However, these measures were sufficient interventions in themselves to effect change in the client system. The values of openness and honesty in confronting process problems, together with the necessary skills, were sufficiently developed in the team not to require further help. The assignment was perhaps one of the shortest in history. The final two stages of PC, evaluation and disengagement, were completed at the end of the meeting and my involvement came to an end. I was and still am confident that the team would in fact integrate their new member and develop new and more appropriate norms of behaviour. This in turn would lead to continuing effective functioning and performance of the Department.

SUMMARY

The three methodologies described in this chapter illustrate the nature of OD in practice. They also show the wide range of approaches available and the suitability of HRM/HRD practitioners to act as OD consultants. One example of acting in an OD consultant role is when working with groups. This can have two common applications: first in leading formal develop-ment groups, and second in team development activities. We will examine each of these applications in Chapters 7 to 9. We now turn to an examination of 'the learning organization'.

6. The learning organization

The term 'learning organization' has achieved common usage in management theory and practice. It is of particular interest to this book for a number of reasons. First, because development and application of the concept is in response to the challenge of continuous change and the need for effective change management (Moss-Jones, 1994). Second, because it arguably represents the most recent articulation of both the goals and processes of organization development. Finally, because, as the term suggests, it is a concept of particular relevance and interest to HRD practitioners. In summary, the application of the concept is a legitimate contribution by development specialists to the management of change through facilitating organization development.

BACKGROUND

The concept of the learning organization is not easy to define or describe. This is because it is still a relatively new idea and, that being the case, it is subject to competing formulations and ongoing debate. Locating its major theoretical origins and influences is a helpful starting point in coming to understand the meaning of the concept.

There are arguably three major influences on definitions and formulations of the learning organization. One of particular importance is the view of organizations as open systems, and the arguments associated with socio-technical analysis. This supports the importance attached to both the focus on people in organizations and the need for systems thinking (Senge, 1991). A second key influence has been theory concerned with 'double loop' learning. Writers such as Argyris and Schon (1978) have developed the original thinking of Bateson (1972) who argued a distinction between learning within a given frame of reference, (single loop learning), and learning which questions, challenges and changes the frame of reference itself (double loop learning). This set of ideas also emphasizes the importance of learning to learn. We will examine a more recent formulation of double loop learning later in this chapter. The third influence is a set of ideas suggesting links between HRD, strategic management and organization success. The argument here is that development and exploitation of core competences through individual and organizational learning is a key factor in achieving competitive advantage (Fredericks and Stewart, 1996).

DEFINITIONS

These influences can usefully be borne in mind when examining and analysing definitions of the learning organization. A definition which is often quoted and which is perhaps better known than most is that offered by Pedler and his co-workers (1991) which arose out of their research into the learning company. The definition is as follows:

'A Learning Company is one which facilitates the learning of all its members, and which continuously transforms itself.'

The use of the word 'company' in this definition is specific to Pedler and his colleagues. It is not, however, meant to refer to profit making organizations or to exclude those from the public and voluntary sectors. The use of the concept of 'company' rather than organization is intended to emphasize collectivity and community as desirable features of work organizations. In other words, it reflects a view of organizations as comprising human social systems which exist to serve common interests through cooperative effort. Thus, the term is consonant with the ideas encapsulated in socio-technical analysis and the values of organization development.

Also explicit in the definition is a focus on individual learning as a feature of the learning organization. More implicit is the notion of this being a continuous process rather than a series of unrelated or unconnected events. The latter may be a view of learning more readily associated with traditional approaches to training and development in work organizations. The reference to continuous transformation is perhaps reflective of double loop learning. What is suggested by the phrase is an organization which does not become trapped into a single frame of reference, or paradigm, and one which is able to adapt and change the assumptions, values and beliefs which underpin its structures, culture and operations. Thus the ability to manage fundamental change is a key feature of the learning organization. A factor not stated and therefore not addressed in the definition is that of strategic success. However, the rationale for pursuing the ideas of the learning company put forward by Pedler *et al* make it clear that our third influencing factor is significant.

A second commonly quoted definition is that provided by Peter Senge (1990). Senge's work has been highly influential in recent organization and management theory, and many of his ideas and prescriptions inform current practice. He defines a learning organization as one where:

> *'People continually expand their capacity to create the results they truly desire, where new and expansive patterns of thinking are nurtured, where collective aspiration is set free, and where people are continually learning to learn together.'*

There are some clear similarities between this definition and that of the learning company. Both focus on continuous individual learning, though Senge has a direct reference to learning to learn. Both assume the possibility and promote the desirability of collective goals achieved through cooperation, though again Senge is more explicit. Senge's definition has a more direct, though still implicit, reference to strategic success through mention of 'results' and 'aspiration'. The major difference is the introduction of 'patterns of thinking' which Senge develops further in his work on systems thinking. We will examine this idea in more detail later in the chapter.

Many other definitions have been offered and could be examined. However, for our purposes I consider just one more worthy of mention. This is provided by Garvin (1993) and again is one which has gained currency in management thought and writing:

> *'A learning organisation is an organisation skilled at creating, acquiring and transferring knowledge, and at modifying its behaviour to reflect new knowledge and insights.'*

This definition is of interest for a number of reasons. First, it focuses on 'behaviour' and thus is in line with the argument of this book as a whole. Organizational learning is about changing organization behaviour. Second, it implies that organizations have skills, an essential one being that of learning. This is resonant with the influencing idea of core competence and competitive advantage. Third, it focuses on 'transferring knowledge'. This is one of the key issues in ideas surrounding the learning organization, especially in terms of translating individual learning into organization learning. Finally, the use of concepts such as 'skills', 'knowledge' and 'modifying behaviour' indicate a language suggestive of HRD practice.

Thus, Garvin's definition (perhaps more explicitly than others) locates the concept within the ambit of HRD practitioners.

FEATURES OF LEARNING ORGANIZATIONS

These definitions provide an indication of what a learning organization might be in practice. They suggest some of the features that might be present. In doing so, they provide a target of what to aim for to become a learning organization, and a benchmark against which to assess current organization practice. However, they are extremely generalized and application of the definitions alone will be very difficult. As Campbell and Cairns (1994) argue, creation of a learning organization requires positive management which, in turn, requires the ability to measure in order to assess, plan and monitor progress. Therefore, there is a need to operationalize the definitions into more specific features which characterize in more measurable terms the nature of the learning organization. This section will provide some ideas on those features which, in turn, can form the basis of measurable descriptors.

General features

There are, in my view, four general features which need to be developed in order to create a learning organization (Stewart, 1994a). The first is an organization which is populated by individuals who are both committed to and have the ability to manage their own development. It is difficult to say that this must be true of all organization members. However, it is equally difficult to say how many or what proportion should display such characteristics. Suffice it to say that the characteristic needs to be generally true. The methods and approaches to individual development described later in the book can be useful in creating this first condition.

A second feature is the existence of processes and methods which encourage and support mutual learning. This refers to enabling and facilitating group-based and team learning. Many of the OD based interventions described in earlier chapters and the later chapters dealing with teams and team development are relevant to developing this feature. It is also a feature emphasized by Senge (1990).

Individual and group, or team, learning, though, are not enough to build a learning organization. Also required are methods and processes which facilitate dissemination and sharing of learning more widely in the organization. This is a feature which is particularly emphasized by Jashpara (1993) as critical for developing a learning organization. How to achieve it is also the subject of some suggestions by Pedler *et al* described below.

None of these features are either likely or sufficient without an appropriate organization culture. This leads to the final general feature of a culture and management style which is supportive of experimentation, risk taking, involvement and independence on the part of employees at all levels. An organization which engenders dependence, control and conformity will not be compatible with the concept of the learning organization. Thus the final feature of an appropriate organization culture is perhaps the most important.

Directors who think

The work of Bob Garratt (1988) is relevant here. Garratt was one of the first writers to use the term 'learning organization' in his work on the need for and nature of development for top managers at director level. He characterizes directors as the 'business brain' whose primary role is to provide direction to and for the organization. This role includes developing appropriate structures and processes that support the kind of style and culture described above. Central to this is the need for directors to have a 'hands-off' approach to operations and to concentrate their attention on the long-term future and survival of the organization in its changing and shifting operating environment.

Garratt also developed a version and representation of double loop learning. His model is useful and practical because it suggests ways of linking both the formal and informal aspects of organizations, and individuals to organization learning. The model is illustrated in Figure 6.1.

The work of Senge

Peter Senge (1990), in his influential work on the learning organization, also suggests a number of features that need to be developed. He argues five characteristics are essential.

The first is referred to as 'personal mastery'. This idea is similar in intent to the feature of committed and able self-developers. It encompasses continuous improvement in learning skills and abilities, as well as notions of continuous personal and professional development. It can also be seen as linked to ideas on self-actualization and achieving potential. The argument is that as potential is achieved it is further developed and, therefore, personal mastery is a continuous process. Senge argues that organizations that aspire to become learning organizations need to support development and application of personal mastery among organization members.

Senge's second feature is that of 'shared vision'. This feature is implicit in his definition given earlier. Unlike some other writers who use similar language, Senge highlights difficulties with 'topdown' vision statements

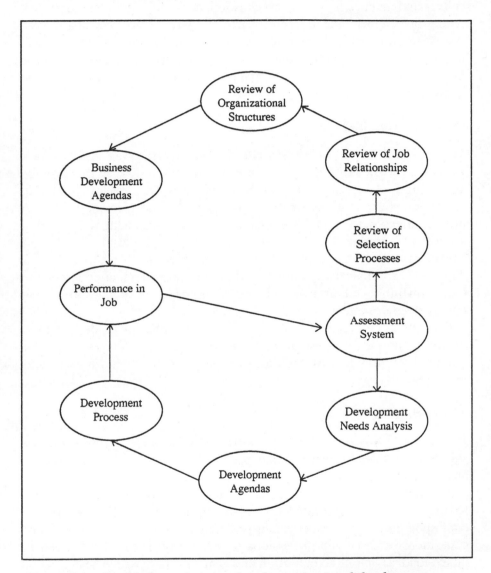

Figure 6.1 *Double loop of personal and organizational development (Source:* Garratt, 1988. With kind permission of Fontana/Collins.)

which are, he says, unlikely to gain commitment. This is an important point. The first requirement in building a shared vision is that individuals are encouraged to hold and to express their own personal vision. The second is that these are the focus of constant discussion and debate as a way of building genuinely shared visions which, themselves, are continually reviewed.

The next feature is resonant of mutual learning. It is referred to as 'team learning'. Senge argues that teams, rather than individuals, are the basic learning unit in modern organizations. This is related to the emerging role of teams as key decision-making forums. In describing team learning, an important distinction is drawn between 'discussion' and 'dialogue'. In some respects, the distinction can be likened to single and double loop learning since discussion is concerned with specific solutions to particular problems, while dialogue is concerned with examining current assumptions and paradigms. Dialogue also requires 'win-win' approaches and a collegial spirit on the part of all team members.

A major focus of Senge's work is what he refers to as 'mental models'. Awareness of their existence, and a willingness to examine and challenge them, is the fourth feature of a learning organization. Mental models consist of the assumptions that govern individuals' and organizations' decisions and actions. An essential characteristic of learning organizations is the ability to formulate alternative perspectives and characterizations of their business and the world in which they operate.

The final feature is what Senge refers to as the 'fifth discipline'. This is concerned with developing systems thinking, which is considered the cornerstone of a learning organization. Systems thinking is concerned with working hard at understanding the complex interrelationships of the modern world, and at identifying causal relationships which influence and affect the behaviour and success (or otherwise!) of work organizations. Senge argues that managers too often focus on single effects and view these as symptoms to be treated. What is required instead is a willingness to examine the 'big picture' in order to establish the true cause or problem.

These five characteristics are the features that Senge argues are associated with a learning organization. They are not separate or independent and all are necessary to the condition of being a learning organization. A more recent book by Senge and his co-authors (Senge *et al*, 1994) provides examples of practical activities and advice on how to develop the features. The features described in the next section are perhaps more directly applicable.

The learning company

Pedler *et al*, (1991) suggest eleven features or characteristics that will be present in a learning organization. They are as follows:

1. The learning approach to strategy.
2. Participative policy making.
3. Informating.
4. Formative accounting and control.
5. Internal exchange.
6. Reward flexibility.
7. Enabling structures.
8. Boundary workers as environmental scanners.
9. Inter-company learning.
10. Learning climate.
11. Self-development opportunities for all.

Each of these is described in more detail in the original work, which also includes some descriptors which can be used as indicators, or measures, of current organization state and progress towards becoming a learning organization. The following paragraphs provide some elaboration and relate the model to the other ideas described here.

The first two elements are resonant with the nature of appropriate organization style and culture described earlier. They suggest the importance of involvement and experimentation. They are also supportive of Senge's arguments on the need for, and processes to achieve, a shared vision. Items three and four in the list are similar in intent to processes for mutual learning and disseminating and sharing learning. The approaches advocated by Pedler *et al* under the headings of 'informating' and 'formative accounting' would help achieve those conditions. Achievement and application of Senge's ideas on team learning would also be relevant here. 'Internal exchange' can also be seen as associated with sharing learning. It may also be supportive of Senge's desire for the surfacing of mental models.

'Reward flexibility' can be a misleading term. It does not necessarily refer to providing incentives for flexible behaviour. The main point is to have flexibility in reward systems so that as conditions and requirements change, so can the incentives and the behaviour which receives reward. This is important in relation to organization culture, and in responding to the results of applying systems thinking. So too is the seventh feature, 'enabling structures'. Rigid and bureaucratic control systems will not facilitate changed behaviour through organization learning.

Item eight, which refers to boundary workers, is of particular interest. The argument is that those in contact with external agents, eg, customers, suppliers, competitors, are ideally placed to act as gatherers of information and intelligence. This is probably true of all organizations, yet such data is rarely shared or utilized. This kind of data will, however, be vital for informing, in Senge's terms, examination of mental models and application of systems thinking. Such data will also be of unique value in supporting directors performing the role suggested by Garratt. These points are also applicable in relation to inter-company learning. The idea here is engaging in mutual learning with suppliers, customers and competitor organizations.

A learning climate is an essential characteristic of culture within a learning organization. It will require support for experimentation and a lack of a 'blame' orientation. In most organizations, achieving such a climate is likely to require an examination of current mental models. It will need to be supported by a genuine shared vision and will be more likely to occur where there is team learning.

The final feature suggested by Pedler and his colleagues has obvious connections to the ideas discussed earlier. It is resonant with the idea of an organization populated by self-developers, and it will be supportive of encouraging personal mastery. When applied throughout the organization, including Directors and other senior managers, it will meet the arguments advanced by Garratt. The opportunities though, and the commitment to maximize them, have to be genuine.

SUMMARY

The concept of The Learning Organization can be said to represent the ultimate articulation of organization development. A variety of specifications, definitions and prescriptions exist for becoming a learning organization. Many of the leading ideas though have a common theoretical base and, relatedly, have many similar features. They also have the common justification or aim of supporting and facilitating the management of organization change, and a common focus on achieving this through learning. Thus, the learning organization represents a set of ideas of relevance and applicability to the practice of HRD.

The central ideas in characterizing a learning organization focus, as does this book, on the three levels of organization, team and individual. Having already considered the first of these, the following chapters focus on team and individual learning.

7. Theories of groups and teams

It is a simple truism of training practice that the 'raw material' that trainers work with is a group of people. Certainly most interventions conducted by training specialists will include some activities which occur in a group context. The membership of the groups may be drawn from a wide range of departments within the organization or may be limited to an actual, intact work team. There are therefore two critical applications of an understanding of group theory by trainers. The first is in providing team development services. This can often form part of or be the central methodology in OD programmes. The second application is when the trainer is engaged in direct training activities with a learning group whose membership is not limited to a particular team. Such activities themselves can be of two types. They may be part of an organization change programme or merely be undertaken to provide the normal maintenance of the organization's skill requirements. Even in this latter case the training experience of learners will have consequences for organization change. This is because the experience will impact on the participants' perceptions of and attitudes towards the organization, the informal relationships in Herman's model given in Chapter 4.

Training specialists need to have a sound understanding of groups and teams if they are to contribute effectively to managing change. This chapter addresses that understanding by concentrating on the theoretical base which underpins sound training practice with groups. The two chapters which follow examine the two major applications of facilitating learning groups and team development.

DEFINING/IDENTIFYING A GROUP

A group is something distinctive from a collection of individuals. Theories of group behaviour suggest three characteristics which are inherent in groups:

- Individuals are aware of each other.

- There is some level of social interaction between members.
- The group has a common objective.

The first two characteristics are commonly true of, say, a bus queue. It might be argued that the third is also true – all members want to catch a bus to reach a destination. Because of this, some writers rely on the collection of individuals to determine for themselves whether or not they are a group. Thus, one definition of a group is as follows:

*A group is any collection of people who **perceive** themselves to be a group.*

The condition implicit in the definition is not likely to be true of the bus queue. Its members individually or collectively would not normally perceive themselves as a group and therefore the queue would not be defined as a group. This raises the question then of what conditions are necessary for the perception to exist. The definition is a valid and accurate description of a group. It implies though that a group exists because individual members identify with the entity of the group which exists outside of themselves. So, why is it that individuals identify with a group and therefore perceive its existence?

The condition of a common objective

The answer to the question is fairly simple. It lies in the third characteristic given earlier: a group has a *common* objective. The bus queue does not. Its members happen to have the same *individual* objective. This is not the same thing as a common objective. In organizational terms a common objective might be to maximize the performance, however measured, of a particular section. This objective is common because it cannot be achieved by a single individual but requires the collective effort of all. The same can be true of a learning group whose common objective may be to maximize the learning of each member.

The existence of a common objective then is the key characteristic of a group. Its existence, however, while a necessary condition is not itself sufficient. In order to meet the definition given above, the members of the group have to accept and identify with the common objective, otherwise they will not perceive themselves to be a group. The challenge for organizations and trainers is to develop a collection of individuals into a group through building acceptance of and identification with a set of common objectives. It is through this process that individuals perceive themselves to be members of a group. There is one final point on the relationship between objectives and groups. As well as a common objective, individuals will also have their own personal objectives which are likely to differ in varying degrees from those of other individuals. The extent to which achievement of individual objectives is facilitated by or dependent upon group membership will also significantly influence the degree of identification with the group. This factor, therefore, will also impact upon the definition of a group being met. These arguments underpin the contemporary interest in culture change or culture management programmes (Anthony, 1994).

The issue of size

One significant issue to do with groups is that of size. Some writers believe that size itself is a key factor in defining a group as distinct from a collection of individuals. This is because size will have a bearing on whether or not the characteristics of awareness and interaction can be operated. Obviously, the larger the number of individuals the more difficult it is for each to be aware of and interact with others. The application of this principle is quite clear in the two contexts of interest to us in this part of the book. The idea of span of control in organization design which suggests limits on the number of staff managed by or reporting to one position is a practical application of the principle. So is the conventional wisdom governing the size of learning groups. In training settings a figure of 20 is normally considered an absolute maximum to achieve effectiveness. Some may suggest an even lower figure of 15 or 12. In educational settings where significantly larger groups are the norm much use is made of small-group or syndicate-based learning methods to overcome problems associated with size. Certainly there will be an optimum number to enable awareness and interaction.

There are two factors which are thought to be important in determining optimum size for a group. The first argues for smaller numbers and the need for participation and involvement. This will build identification with the common objectives and therefore with the group. The second argues in favour of larger numbers and the need for a broad base of knowledge and expertise. This will help ensure a higher quality and quantity of task achievement. Higher numbers may also be desirable for reasons of representing all legitimate interests in groups such as committees or working parties. The optimum for any particular group therefore will be a balance of these factors.

Is size relevant?
An alternative view of size is possible. It is that size is irrelevant so long as identification with common objectives is present. Such a view is consistent with the definition of a group given in the last section: so long as all members perceive themselves to be a group then the group exists. This is significant for organizations. Operationally, the 'group' known as XYZ Manufacturing Company can be said to exist if all organization members accept and identify with the common objectives. No matter what the size therefore, whether it is tens or hundreds or thousands, an organization can be a group. The same is true of sub-units of organizations, eg, divisions or departments. This is only one reason why organizations have a concern to build an understanding of and commitment to their objectives in all employees. Training has an obvious contribution in this process through arrangements for inducting and orienting new employees. All training experiences, irrespective of their overt purpose, impact on the process through influencing individual perceptions and attitudes.

To summarize so far, a group can be of any size so long as its members perceive themselves to be a group. The critical factor in this perception is acceptance of and identification with common objectives; awareness of and interaction with other members are also significant factors. Indeed, interaction with others can build acceptance and identification. The descriptions of groups which follow assume this definition.

OPERATING DYNAMICS OF GROUPS

One theory of group dynamics distinguishes between two separate ingredients in the workings of a group. One is labelled 'content' and is to do with the purpose or task of the group. This means *what* the group needs or wishes to get done. The second is labelled 'process' and this refers to *how* the group achieves its purpose or accomplishes its task.

Group processes

Process in this sense does not refer to a technical means or system of carrying out work such as a production process based on an assembly line or an information management process based on a computer system. The meaning of the term is similar but in this case is applied to the means by which the group carries out group tasks such as planning and allocating work, making decisions and solving problems. In other words, process here is the same concept as that applied in Process Consultancy. However, as with a poor quality production or information management process, the output achieved in terms of group tasks will be poor quality if poor quality processes are adopted. A low quality manufacturing process will produce low quality cars. A low quality decision making process will produce low quality decisions.

It should be clear from this that group processes are to do with how the individual members work together and interact with one another in carrying out their tasks. The term 'group dynamics' was coined by Lewin (Bennis, 1976; French, 1984) to describe these processes since they both generate and direct the energy of the group and individual members. However, most individuals most of the time and therefore most groups most of the time focus energy and attention on the 'content' ingredient of their work at the expense of 'process'. Because of this little or no effort is given to ensuring high quality processes are adopted, and most groups most of the time do not achieve the quality of output, ie, 'content' of which they are capable. Some of the critical process issues that groups need to address to ensure high quality are discussed below.

Process issues

- *Participation*

  This refers to levels of participation by individual members of the group. Ideally, the level of participation will meet the requirements of the group and satisfy the individual. However, this is often not the case and groups need to be aware of who is participating and who is not. More important is to identify the reasons for high or low levels of participation and to overcome any non-productive causes.

- *Communication*

  This is often an obvious and easily identified example of poor process. A significant element is the level and quality of listening when the group is working together. Is everyone's attention focused on whoever is speaking? Similarly, do speakers address themselves to and therefore communicate with the whole group or do they focus their remarks on only a minority of members? Related to this is the practice of 'side meetings'. This is where sub-groups of members engage in separate discussions. Looking for and identifying communication patterns within the group through such behaviours can be very revealing of weaknesses in the group's process.

● *Information sharing*
The content of communications is also a significant issue of group process. Free sharing of information is obviously desirable if the group is to be effective. Too often, though, information is seen as power and is held on to by individuals and not shared with other group members.

● *Leadership style*
It is important to recognize that leadership is exercised in all groups. In most cases there will be a formal leader, eg, a manager in relation to a work group or a trainer in relation to a learning group. Where no formal leader exists leadership will be exercised by some or all group members. The style adopted is a critical process issue. An autocratic style is unlikely to create the conditions necessary for identification with the group (see the arguments in support of the Leadership Grid in Chapter 5). A democratic style and one which allows leadership to be shared is considered to produce more effective or higher quality group processes.

● *Influence*
Related to leadership style is the issue of influence. The questions that arise concern who has influence, why, and to what extent influence shifts. Low quality process gives influence to those who speak first or most or loudest. High quality implies that influence shifts on a rational basis, eg, who has experience or skills or relevant information.

● *Decision making*
This is a significant issue and determinant of quality in group process. There is also a strong relationship with leadership style. The first item to be aware of is how effective the group is at recognizing decision points. Often discussion and debate continues unproductively long after a decision could or should have been reached. This is because groups are not skilled at utilizing decision processes and this also explains the second item. This is 'avoidance behaviour' which groups often engage in to put off confronting difficult decisions. The final item relates to adopting appropriate decision making processes. There is no one right way for groups to make decisions. It depends on the nature of the decision and particularly the effect it will have on group members.

● *Feelings*
The final key process issue is how the group deals with members' feelings. The first concern is the extent to which members feel free in expressing

their feelings. This applies to both positive feelings such as enjoyment and pride as well as negative feelings such as frustration or anger. A second concern is handling conflict. It is a truism that when two or more individuals work together there is likely to be conflict, eg, differences of objectives, opinions or priorities. Conflict can be seen as a negative force and therefore suppressed. This usually leads to unproductive outcomes. Conversely, conflict can be seen as a positive force and its open expression and resolution as leading to higher quality outcomes. Productive conflict resolution is the ideal in terms of an effective group process.

All of the above issues critically affect the quality of group processes and therefore the quality of group tasks. An effective group is one which is aware of and consciously manages the issues to ensure high quality processes.

PROCESS FUNCTIONS

The processes described in the preceding list represent the collective behaviours of individual group members in the way they work together. Such behaviours serve two separate but related functions. Each function is essential for effective group working. Group processes can be distinguished according to the function they perform. There are those which contribute to achieving the work of the group: *Task Functions*, and those which build, maintain and develop group cohesiveness: *Maintenance Functions*.

Task functions

Task functions include the following:

- *Information giving/seeking*
  This refers to sharing information related to the task with all group members. It also includes asking questions of other group members to solicit information.

- *Making proposals*
  These behaviours relate to offering suggestions on matters such as planning and organizing tasks, allocating work, setting objectives and prioritizing.

- *Summarizing discussions*
  This can occur at any point during group meetings and need not occur

exclusively at the end. Keeping group members informed of where they have got to at regular intervals can be beneficial in reaching sound conclusions.

● *Evaluating*
It is essential that ideas and proposals are assessed as to their suitability. Often, a number of options need to be considered before a final decision is taken. Evaluating refers to behaviours which help perform these functions.

● *Giving direction*
This item refers to providing leadership within the group. Such behaviours are not normally the exclusive preserve of the formal leader in an effectively functioning group.

These behaviours contribute to achieving the tasks required of a group. However, groups also require that sound relationships are formed and that members gain personal satisfaction from their membership. Behaviours which contribute to that ensure cohesiveness within the group. These are the maintenance functions described below.

Maintenance functions

● *Encouraging participation*
Inviting other members to express their views and opinions, checking out understanding and agreement, requesting advice and contributions from others all of these behaviours encourage participation and thereby contribute to cohesiveness in a group.

● *Communicating/listening*
Being a good listener, not interrupting and paying attention to whoever speaks in group meetings all demonstrate genuine valuing of each member and thus build sound relationships. Addressing verbal contributions to all members and not particular individuals in group meetings has similar effects.

● *Relieving tension*
As indicated earlier, conflict is inevitable in groups and can lead to tension, especially when making difficult decisions. Taking the heat out of such moments through a light-hearted or humorous remark can relieve the tension and help maintain sound relationships.

- *Building trust*

  This is a critical aspect of the maintenance functions. Behaviours which demonstrate trust in the group and/or individual members will have the effect of developing trust as a group norm. This is an important feature of cohesive and effective groups. Accepting the judgement of others, delegating tasks, taking direction, are examples of behaviours which demonstrate trust.

- *Observing process*

  Being aware of, observing and providing feedback on process issues is a final example of maintenance functions. It is a function often performed initially by an external facilitator such as a Process Consultant. It is, though, an important function which needs to be performed throughout the life of a group so that process problems which threaten cohesiveness or task completion can be identified and resolved.

Applying the concepts

This analysis of process functions is helpful for a number of reasons. It highlights what needs to happen in groups in order for them to operate effectively. This is not confined only to when the group is working as a whole, for example at group meetings. The same is true when group members are working singly, in pairs or in sub-groups on tasks which form part of the group's overall work. Many of the functions can and need to be performed in those contexts. This point is obviously significant when thinking about a total organization as a group. The analysis is still relevant in those circumstances. It provides a useful description of the desired approach to managing organizations and a framework for diagnosing possible causes of dysfunctioning. The analysis also tells us that an effective group has within its membership individuals both able and willing to perform all of the required functions.

Obviously no single individual will be expected to exhibit behaviours associated with all of the task and maintenance functions. Individual differences in personality, temperament, experience and skills lead to different natural preferences of behaviour and therefore contributions in terms of process functions. What is critical is that all of the functions are performed through the individual contributions of all group members. A lack of contribution in important areas, especially the maintenance functions, is often the cause of ineffectiveness in groups. The role of a Process Consultant, discussed in Chapter 5, can often be to help a group identify and overcome such deficiencies. This can be aided in turn by observing and analysing individual contributions using a framework such as that given in Figure 7.1.

	Group Members					
Task Behaviours						
Information/Opinion Giver						
Information/Opinion Seeker						
Starter/Proposer						
Direction Giver/Organizer						
Summarizer						
Coordinator						
Diagnoser of Task Problems						
Evaluator						
Maintenance Behaviours						
Encourager of Participation						
Harmonizer/Compromiser						
Tension Reliever						
Communication Helper						
Evaluator of Emotional Climate						
Process Observer						
Standard Setter						
Active Listener						
Trust Builder						
Interpersonal Problem Solver						

Figure 7.1 *Process observation sheet*

95

FEATURES OF EFFECTIVE GROUPS

The description of group theory so far gives some useful indicators of the kinds of characteristics exhibited by effective groups, and, therefore, what features need to be developed to maximize effectiveness. First, effective groups are aware of and pay attention to their own process. This involves continuous monitoring and review leading to improvements in processes adopted. Second, and as part of process review, they ensure that both task and maintenance functions are performed. Third and critically, effective groups have among their membership individuals who are skilled at group working and are able to develop similar skills in others. This is the ultimate aim of PC.

Critical features

The critical process issues identified earlier also manifest themselves in certain ways. The following list describes the features of effective groups in terms of those process issues:

- *Objectives*
  These are very clear to all group members and to a large extent are shared, that is, agreed with and supported, by all members.

- *Communication*
  This is effective and includes feelings as well as content items such as task-related information.

- *Leadership*
  This is not held on to by the formal leader but is widely distributed and shared among all members. A participative style such as the 9.9 orientation of Blake and Mouton (see Chapter 5) is adopted.

- *Influence*
  The exercise of influence within the group shifts according to a rational basis such as information or expertise.

- *Conflict*
  This is seen as a natural consequence of involvement. Lack of conflict would be a cause of concern since it would suggest lack of involvement. Conflict is openly expressed and resolved, and seen as a positive source of higher quality solutions.

- *Decision making*
  Generally decisions are reached on the basis of open debate though processes are amended according to the nature of the decision and its impact on or importance to group members. To take an example from training, most participants would accept it as appropriate for the Trainer to decide alone to delay a break by 15 minutes. They would not, though, have the same view of a decision to delay a planned finishing time by two hours!

- *Interpersonal relationships*
  These are emphasized as being important to group cohesiveness. Each individual group member is valued equally for their unique contribution to the group.

- *Monitoring and review*
  Group working and processes are continuously monitored and regularly reviewed. Evaluation of effectiveness is a feature of how the group works.

The list of features can be applied to any group. It can be a learning group, an intact work team, a management team or a whole organization. It again provides the basis for diagnosing weaknesses in group effectiveness. The aim in improving effectiveness will be to bring those features about in the group being examined. At an organization level, it can be argued that OD in general and programmes such as the Leadership Grid have the creation of these features as their ultimate goal, since they represent a way of managing and working which facilitates learning and effective management of change.

The question which naturally arises from this argument is how to develop the features. The three methodologies discussed in Chapter 5 provide some answers, and other ideas are examined in more detail in the following two chapters. A further theory of groups and the way they develop is of relevance in examining the question.

A MODEL OF GROUP DEVELOPMENT

This model of group development is based on the work of Tuckman (Ribeaux, 1978) who suggested that groups experience five stages:

- Forming
- Storming

- Norming
- Performing
- Ending

The first four stages are those normally focused on since the final stage is only relevant to groups with a finite life. Such groups in organizations are confined to project teams, working parties, steering committees and the like which are brought together for a specific purpose and disband when the purpose is achieved. Most groups in work organizations are ongoing and remain in existence even though their membership may change, eg, a management team or particular section in a department.

The operation of Tuckman's four stages of development can usefully be distinguished according to how they impact on the task and maintenance functions identified earlier; Figure 7.2 gives a summary of the results.

Forming

During the *forming* stage when the group first comes together members are highly dependent on some 'other' person, normally the formal leader, to provide structure in terms of how they should relate to each other. This includes setting the agenda and establishing ground rules of behaviour. On the task side the goal or objective needs to be clarified, the issues to be considered need specifying and an understanding of the work provided. In summary, there is a need for orientation. The issues that concern group members during this stage, therefore, are questions such as what, why and how.

Storming

The second stage of *storming* occurs when some of these initial questions have begun to be answered. In terms of maintenance functions there is likely to be a great deal of conflict. Much of this conflict is to do with challenging formal authority to test the limits, sorting out acceptable and workable 'pecking orders' among those of equal formal status, and settling differences of view on ground rules of behaviour. The task functions are to do with sorting out who does what, what rewards will be available and what criteria will be applied in their application. In other words, the concern is with getting organized to deal with the work of the group. The focus of attention is leadership and power within the group.

It may be useful to emphasize at this point that actual work can and usually does get done throughout all four stages. Even during the first two

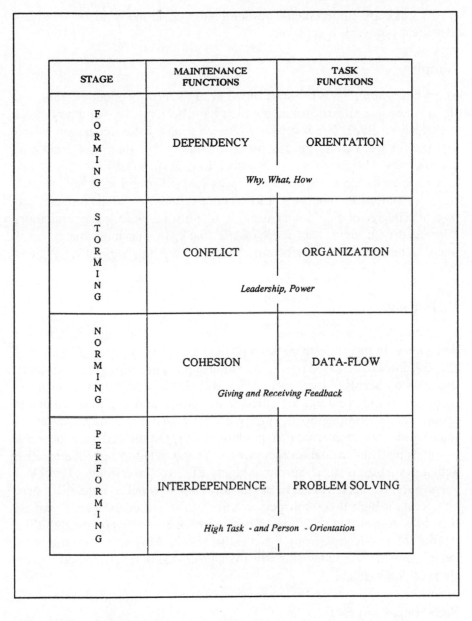

Figure 7.2 *A model of group development*

stages tasks are undertaken and completed. It is likely to be relatively inefficient but work is achieved.

Norming

Stage three, *norming*, is the start of the group's most productive work. On the maintenance side the initial conflicts have been resolved and new issues are openly resolved. The group has in this stage established an identity which separates it from other groups for its members and there is a feeling of togetherness. The group is now cohesive. In relation to task functions there is a high exchange and sharing of ideas and information, together with mutual exploration of options and decisions on action. This is characterized by a high degree of data flow. Cutting across both functions are behaviours concerned with giving and receiving feedback. In this stage the group is likely to be adequately performing both maintenance and task functions described earlier.

Performing

From the third stage the group will progress naturally with little effort to *performing*. In this stage there is a high degree of trust between all members expressed in an increased use of individuals, pairs and sub-groups to carry out tasks on behalf of the group. There will also be a high commitment by members to the common activities of the group and support within the group for experimentation. This is characterized by a high degree of interdependence in internal group relationships. On the task side the work is well defined, functional competence has been developed and collaborative activities are the norm. The group is highly efficient and effective at problem solving and therefore is able to handle any change which is required. There is, overall, a high task- and person-orientation within the group and its members. A group at this stage of development is very likely to exhibit the features of an effective group listed earlier; or, looking at it from the other perspective, in order to become effective a group has to reach the performing stage of development.

Some important factors

There are a number of factors to understand about the operation of these stages. First, they are necessarily sequential. This means that the third stage, for example, cannot be reached without progressing through stages one and two. Second, progression through the stages is not automatic or inevitable.

Groups can and often do remain in stages one or two and never develop to stages three or four. Third, while the stages are sequential and therefore time-bound, it is not possible to generalize on time-scales. A group may take hours, days, weeks or even months or years to progress from stage one to stage four, or remain stuck in stage two for their whole life. Fourth, whenever a member leaves and is replaced by a new individual, by definition this is a new group. The group therefore returns to stage one in its development.

In broad terms a group requires skilled members to progress to stage four – skilled in terms of understanding and utilizing group dynamics. This can often form the basis of a PC assignment, although it cannot be said that specialist PC activities are a requirement in all cases. This theory of group development has many other applications for Trainers in managing change which will be examined in later chapters. There are two other theoretical bases for group dynamics relevant to training practitioners.

AN ALTERNATIVE THEORY OF GROUPS

One of these theories focuses on the needs of individuals in examining what makes for effective groups. The notion is simply one of suggesting that groups will be effective to the extent that they satisfy the needs of their members. This idea is not inconsistent with the theories described so far. Individuals are probably more likely to identify with and be committed to a group which satisfies their personal needs than to one which does not. Such identification and commitment will lead to cohesiveness within the group which in turn will lead to effectiveness. Indeed, a cohesive group can be defined as one which individuals enjoy and wish to remain in. This condition is more likely to be true if the group meets individual needs.

Individual needs

There are three types of needs that individuals seek to have satisfied through group membership:

- *Belonging or affiliation*
  This is expressed through the need for *inclusion* which means feeling part of and valued by the group.

- *Power or influence*
  This refers to the need to feel that the individual can influence the

direction and decisions of the group, expressed through the need for *control*.

● *Affection or love*
This is expressed through the need for *affection* which means being able to both express and give as well as receive affection with other group members.

Needless to say individuals will vary in the importance they attach to each of these needs. Some individuals, for example, will need more control and others more affection. What is important is that a group enables each of its members to meet their needs to whatever extent is required to satisfy them.

It should be apparent that groups which achieve this are also most likely to exhibit the features of effectiveness listed earlier.

A THEORY OF EFFECTIVE TEAMS

All that has been described so far can be applied to teams in work organizations. An effective team will be an effective group and vice versa. The final theory I wish to describe in this chapter is one specially devoted to work teams, in particular management teams. The theory was developed by Belbin (1981), a British researcher who has been a leading writer on training and development for many years.

The nature of the theory

The basic propositions of this theory are not dissimilar to the ideas described earlier. First, teams require certain functions to be performed if they are to be effective. Second, these functions need to be fulfilled by team members adopting appropriate and complementary roles within the team. Third, individuals will naturally adopt a particular role for reasons of personality and ability.

Belbin identifies eight possible team roles based on broad personality types. These are listed with a short description of each in Figure 7.3. Assessment of any particular individual's preferred or natural team role is through one of two means. A rigorous assessment is through use of personality measurement instruments; Cattel's 16 PF or the Saville & Holdsworth OPQ have both been validated for the purpose; and an intelligence measurement instrument, usually the Watson-Glazer CTA. The

Chairman	-	Ensures objectives are clear. Ensures all contributions are considered. Keeps team on track.
Shaper	-	Challenges inertia. Provides drive and direction. Achievement - and task - oriented.
Company Worker	-	Undertakes task related work. Well organized. Disciplined and reliable.
Plant	-	Creative. Generates ideas. Provides alternatives and questions assumptions.
Team Worker	-	Process - and people - oriented. Promotes team spirit. Sensitive to team needs and climate.
Resource Investigator	-	Acts as contact with external environment. Provides knowledge of 'who' and 'what'. Effective negotiator with external agents.
Monitor-Evaluator	-	Practical orientation. Provides realistic assessments/evaluations. Concerned with what works.
Completer-Finisher	-	Attention to detail. Conscientious in meeting targets/deadlines. Concerned to achieve steady/ measurable progress.

Figure 7.3 *Team skills management – the eight roles (Source:* Bebin, 1989. With kind permission of Butterworth-Heinemann (Oxford) Ltd.*)*

second means is through self-assessment and assessment by others which is scored through a computer programme.

The major premise of Belbin's theory is that an effective team needs to be balanced in terms of the roles performed by its members. Essentially, a team requires all of the roles to be adopted in order for all of the required functions to be performed. There is one exception. An effective team requires either a Chairman or a Shaper but not both. This is because such roles clash with one another. An effective team also requires only one Shaper for similar reasons – more than one will lead to non-productive conflict. That exception aside, an effective team *must* have persons performing each of the roles and can afford to have duplication.

Using the theory

This major premise has been well demonstrated by extensive research and development by Belbin and his colleagues. There is an abundance of experimental and empirical evidence to support the assertion of what makes for an effective team. However, Belbin's argument does not mean that teams should have seven members or be composed of carefully selected individuals. Deciding the composition of and selecting members for teams is obviously one application of the theory. However, it is also useful as a diagnostic tool in identifying causes of weaknesses or problems in team functioning, and in providing a framework for deciding on appropriate remedial action to develop increased effectiveness. Few individuals are locked into one team role by fixed personality characteristics, so team members can develop the behaviours of their secondary roles to ensure all functions are performed.

SUMMARY

Applying team skills management to ensure performance of team functions indicates that this theory is also complementary to those described earlier. Indeed, an examination of the team roles in comparison with task and maintenance functions and the features of effective groups shows many similarities. While there may not be a perfect match it is clear nonetheless that all of the theories of groups and teams described contain similar messages for organizations and therefore for HRD practitioners. Particular applications of interest to the latter are in facilitating learning groups and in providing team development activities. Both are significant in helping to manage change. The former can have an impact on individuals' ability to cope with change as well as occurring as part of change programmes. The latter can constitute the major strategy in OD change programmes or be intended to develop improved ability to manage change. An effective team is a learning team. A learning team is effective in managing change. The next two chapters examine these two major applications of group theories.

8. Facilitating learning groups

Facilitating is a key component of Trainer effectiveness. It is a topic of particular importance when looking at managing change through training and development, because a need for such skills can arise in a number of contexts in relation to managing change in work organizations. The term 'facilitating' is ambiguous and can have different meanings. Indeed, over the last 10 years or so the term can be said to have become overused to the extent of causing unnecessary confusion. I will, therefore, begin this chapter by examining the various contexts in which facilitating can or needs to be applied. From that discussion I will then offer a definition and explanation of the term. These two sections will form a sound base for examining the practical use of facilitating and the associated skills.

THE CONTEXTS OF FACILITATING

There are three broad categories of activity which call for the application and use of facilitating skills in relation to managing change. These are, (1) in implementing OD or other organization change programmes; (2) in providing direct training events as part of change programmes; (3) in the normal maintenance function of training and development. Each of these is considered below.

1. Organization development/change programmes

There are numerous examples in this category. The feedback stage of the Survey Feedback method is one. Specifically the meetings involved in PIMs illustrate the point. Strategy development workshops for top teams and team development in general is another. Many OD/change programmes utilize groups such as Project Teams, Quality Circles, Task Groups, Steering Committees, Working Parties. One recent example I heard of within the finance sector utilized the term 'Change Teams'. Such approaches often require the services of an HRM/HRD specialist to 'facilitate' the work of the groups involved.

It is clear from this list of applications that facilitating will always be a key activity in bringing about organization change. Since HRM and HRD specialists are key personnel in managing such programmes they obviously need a measure of ability in terms of facilitating skills.

2. Change-related direct training events

As we saw in the chapter on Planned Change, training is often a key part of an implementation strategy. This often involves some form of direct training event. A current example in the UK is implementing newly adopted quality management policies.

The critical issue in this context is the approach adopted to such training. Organization members will have their own attitude to the particular change being implemented. The overall implementation strategy will be designed (hopefully) to encourage the adoption of positive attitudes. Training must play its part in that process. Often the change will require not only the development of new knowledge and skills but the re-examination of current beliefs and values held by individuals. Training, if it is to be relevant, must enable that to happen.

The adoption of positive attitudes to a given change and examination of current beliefs and values cannot be achieved through traditional direct training methods; other methods and techniques need to be adopted. The kinds of methods which are appropriate require Trainers to act as 'facilitators' rather than teachers or instructors passing on expert knowledge and skills. Thus direct training events provided as part of organization change programmes are a key and critical context for facilitating skills.

3. Maintenance-related direct training events

We have seen that a learning organization is effective in managing change. The provision of training and development has significant impact on creating such an organization merely by doing its traditional job of ensuring requisite knowledge and skills are available within the organization.

No matter what the purpose or content of direct training activities, the learners' experience of training activity will have the following effects.

a. An influence, positive or negative, on the learners' attitude to their job, the organization and the activity of training. From the last will also come attitudes towards further learning.
b. An inherent message about how the individual is viewed by the organization and what is expected of them. The clearest example of this is where direct training events are very formal in their character and

adopt didactic methods and techniques. The 'message' is one of 'someone else knows best' and participants learn dependence on that someone else. The effect of this is to discourage initiative and innovation.

c. An impact on the development of core or transferable skills such as problem solving, decision making, working with others as part of a team and ability to manage own learning.

Depending on the outcomes of these three effects, training can either support and encourage or discourage and suppress commitment to and ability in continuous learning. This will have a direct effect on the individual and the organization. In turn, this effect will help determine the ability of both the individual and the organization to cope with and manage change.

The primary variables which influence the learner's experience of training and determine the effects listed above are first, the methods and techniques used to train and second, the nature of the Trainer Learner relationship. Adopting a facilitating rather than teaching approach to the operation of these two variables is more likely to achieve positive outcomes in terms of the three effects. That is, learners are likely to adopt positive attitudes, learn independence and develop core skills. This will in turn engender and support development of a learning organization, an organization better able to manage change.

This is not to decry or argue against the use of didactic methods and techniques. They are of course wholly appropriate and sometimes essential for many purposes and subjects. I am, however, arguing for some elements of facilitating in terms of both methods and relationships to be incorporated into all direct training events. Through this simple process Trainers have a direct and positive impact on the organization's ability to manage change.

FACILITATING DEFINED

The root word of facilitating is facile. According to the Oxford Dictionary this means 'easy', 'fluent', 'easy-going' and 'flexible'. The action form of the word, ie, facilitate, means to promote or make easy. Essentially then the act of 'facilitating' is to enable something to happen easily. It is not to do the something oneself but to promote the doing of it by others.

In our context the 'something' done by others is learning, or more precisely, the 'something' is changing through and by learning. Facilitating learning groups therefore means enabling change to occur in the individuals and the group. Inherent in this definition is the proposition that learning is not something which can be done to or imposed on people. Facilitating provides the opportunity for learning, promotes its occurrence and seeks to make it easy.

Achieving a facilitating approach

The root word suggests some interesting clues as to how this can be achieved. Its definition uses words such as fluent, flexible and easy-going. These indicate characteristics which need to be present in the person doing the facilitating: the facilitator. In order to be effective in the act of facilitating, the training specialist is required to display those qualities. This implies certain guidelines on the application of the two variables identified earlier. Facilitating learning groups means establishing informal, relaxed relationships within the learning group and between the group and the facilitator. This in turn means developing a cohesive group which is effective in managing process issues. In terms of methods and techniques, the necessity is to enable learning to occur rather than to teach. Methods also need to support the development of effective group processes since the group itself is a major vehicle for individual learning. Flexibility in developing relationships and in using learning methods is also critical. Plans have to be capable of adaptation to meet changing circumstances and demands. To achieve all of this the facilitator needs to be 'fluent' in the use and application of group theories. The following sections concentrate on providing practical advice on these critical aspects of facilitating.

ESTABLISHING AND MAINTAINING AN APPROPRIATE CLIMATE

In all of the three contexts described earlier, the aim of the facilitator is to enable learning to occur. The focus of the learning in each context can be some specific content issue such as a major change in the operating environment and/or the organization itself, or it can be a process issue affecting the working of the group, for example in developing improved decision making procedures in an intact work team. In either case an appropriate climate supportive of individual and group learning needs to be established. Establishing such a climate is part of developing an effective group and therefore it is a matter of modelling appropriate behaviours, meeting individual needs and helping the group through its natural stages of development. All of these can be achieved by utilizing techniques designed to apply what is known from group theory. Two specific techniques are described, followed by a discussion of facilitator behaviours.

1. Ice-breakers

The initial activities of a learning experience are critical in setting the climate for what follows. The use of ice-breakers is designed to establish participation and involvement as the norm. They can also be used for the following purposes:

- To help progress the group through the forming stage quickly.
- To meet individual needs for orientation and inclusion.
- To establish as norms of behaviour characteristics associated with effective groups such as communicating, listening and information sharing.
- To set a climate of openness and cooperation.

Paired introductions   There are a wide variety of ice-breaker activities to choose from. Many focus on participant introductions to the whole group. Depending on the nature of the learning group in terms of whether they are known to each other or not, there are two in particular which I find very effective. The first assumes a learning group of strangers and simply requires participants to work in pairs and to spend five minutes each getting to know their partner. Guidance can be given on what kind of data to ask for, eg, job history, family, hobbies, etc, or such decisions left to the pairs. Following this discussion in pairs each individual then introduces their partner to the whole group.

There is a variation on this which I use if the focus of the learning is to do with issues such as stereotyping, first impressions or perceptions of others. This variation is described in Figure 8.1.

The second paired introduction ice-breaker is for use when members of the group are known to each other. It involves individuals deciding how they would describe their partner as a colour, a make of car and in terms of a fictional character. Similar conditions apply as to the activity in Figure 8.1 in that each pair must share their perceptions with their partners before introductions are made to the whole group. Variations on this activity include changing the focus of the descriptions or directing the gathering of data which is not likely to be known, for example, favourite film star, favourite holiday destination, current and ultimate ambitions. Using this ice-breaker can be very revealing and useful when working with intact work teams as part of team development. It can generate useful data on

---

1. Select a number of factors about individuals, eg:

    Marital status
    Favourite TV show
    Daily newspaper bought or read
    Political party voted for at last election
    Favourite sport or hobby
    Favourite food
    Most respected personal hero

2. Instruct participants to decide and write down answers they think are true of their partner without discussion, ie, they make their choice solely by looking at their partner.

3. Participants then discuss their answers and reasons with their partner and also gather accurate data on these factors.

4. Each participant then introduces their partner to the whole group giving both their initial answers with reasons and the data supplied by their partner.

5. The feelings generated in the paired work and whole group introductions are discussed.

Figure 8.1   *Paired introduction, ice-breaker variant*

perceptions and relationships that exist in the team as well as being a useful indicator of how well team members actually know each other. It can also be very amusing and generate a lot of fun!

Problem solving activities   A second type of ice-breaker engages the group in some form of problem solving activity. This type is not necessarily mutually exclusive with paired introductions and can follow on from that activity. Problem solving activities do have the advantage of requiring a broader range of behaviours associated with effective groups and of creating the potential of progressing the storming stage more quickly. A particular favourite of mine is the Colours Exercise which is described in Figure 8.2. This activity can also be used to create sub-groups required for utilizing the next technique.

Purpose:

1.   To set a climate of active involvement and mutual responsibility.

2.   To enable participants to begin to get to know each other.

3.   To form 3 or 4 small sub-groups.

Procedure:

1.   Pre-prepare individually addressed envelopes containing a card with one printed word linked to a particular colour or theme.

2.   Hand out envelopes and inform participants they have all information required, individually and collectively, to form sub-groups.

3.   Set time limit of say 15-20 minutes for completion.

Conditions:

Composition of sub-groups is pre-determined on arbitrary basis.

Figure 8.2   *The colours exercise*

2. Contract setting exercises

Contract setting is an important activity in creating an appropriate climate. When I talk to other trainers about the use of contract setting a common objection is that it is too time-consuming to use on maintenance-related direct training events. I do not agree. Its use in practice can be amended to suit the time available. A second objection is the scope for flexibility in maintenance-related training which often has very specific objectives. Again I do not accept the objection since the use of contract setting is very flexible and can be tailored to suit specific circumstances. To illustrate that both objections can be overcome I have used contract setting on a one-day letter writing course for administrative staff and many other similar programmes.

It is probably more critical that contract setting exercises are undertaken in the first two contexts described in the first section of the chapter. Team development and direct training events as part of organization change programmes are two particularly important examples. The use of contract setting exercises is designed to achieve the following purposes:

- To help progress new groups through the storming stage.
- To meet individual needs for inclusion and control.
- To establish clear and shared objectives.
- To develop norms associated with effective groups such as shared leadership, consensus decision making, sound interpersonal relationships and conflict resolution.
- To reinforce norms of behaviour such as listening, information sharing and cooperation.

The nature of contract setting   Contract setting exercises and their overt purpose are designed to involve the whole group in agreeing the ground rules for the learning experience. The whole group is taken to include the facilitator. The process usually involves three stages:

1. Individual activity.
2. Small group/syndicate activity.
3. Plenary report back and discussion.

It is during the third stage that facilitators provide their input into the negotiation by confirming what is and is not achievable and acceptable within the context of the programme. Clear guidance should, of course, be given by the facilitator on these issues at the start of the process and in the focus provided for the contract. However, it can happen that syndicates come up with suggestions or proposals that are unrealistic and these must be dealt with rather than ignored. Facilitators may have their own proposals which can be added to those of the group in the plenary if they have not been identified by participants. Confidentiality may be an example. Such proposals need to be accepted and agreed by the group.

A common focus for a contract setting exercise is given in Figure 8.3. Group members are normally provided with a prepared sheet for the individual activity. A second sheet is provided for the syndicate activity. The plenary session consists of each syndicate reporting their conclusions with the use of completed flipcharts. The whole group then discusses each report and agrees a final response to each item. Depending on the nature of the group, eg, existing team, task group, training group, the final item only can be the focus of the agreed contract.

Displaying the contract   The final results form a contract between all involved in the learning experience. As such, the contract should be readily available for reference and therefore a summary flipchart should be posted for the duration of the group's meetings and/or members supplied with a typed copy. It should be emphasized that adherence to the contract by all is an individual and collective responsibility. The facilitator is not the only person responsible for ensuring compliance.

---

1.   **Individual Activity**

Complete the following statements according to your personal feelings about this (programme, activity, group, etc).

A.   I expect to gain:

B.   I intend to contribute:

C.   I expect others to:

D.   The standard of behaviour and speech I wish to have adopted by the group is:

E.   The 'ground rules' I wish to have adopted are:

2.   **Syndicate Activity**

Using the results of the individual activity as a basis for discussion please reach agreement on the following points. Agree a spokesperson to report your conclusions.

A.   Expected gains/objects.

B.   Expected contributions.

C.   Ground rules to be adopted.

Figure 8.3   *Contract setting exercise*

Contract setting is a useful technique for producing shared objectives and ground rules of behaviour which reflect the requirements for effective group functioning. The output of such exercises also provides a useful focus for regular monitoring and review. Depending on the nature and purpose of the group using the technique, the frequency of reference to the contract can be daily, weekly or meeting-by-meeting. Referring to the contract regularly keeps the group on track in the way it tackles its work. It can also help to highlight and tackle process problems as they occur and so prevent serious dysfunctioning. This may involve re-negotiating items in the contract.

3. Facilitator behaviours

Ice-breaker and contract setting exercises are techniques which utilize effective group processes as a means of developing similar processes in the groups which use them. Experiencing the process involved in the techniques enables a group to establish an appropriate climate for learning. This is important to achieve because facilitating, as opposed to teaching or instructing, implies methods which utilize the group as a vehicle for learning and change and therefore requires effective processes within the group. The behaviours adopted and displayed by the facilitator need to reinforce the message.

It can be argued with justification that by utilizing ice-breakers and contract setting exercises the facilitator is modelling appropriate and desired behaviours. This will have an effect on the group and individual members. While this is true, the facilitator needs to be aware of even more specific behaviours which will have equally significant effects. Some examples are listed below:

- Being an effective communicator and addressing contributions to the whole group.
- Demonstrating the above by sharing eye-contact with all members.
- Being a good listener and attending to whoever speaks.
- Demonstrating the above by active listening behaviour such as looking, maintaining eye-contact, reflecting.
- Valuing all group members and their contributions equally.
- Demonstrating the above by acknowledging, welcoming and responding to all contributions.
- Being willing to share leadership and influence within the group.
- Demonstrating the above by, for example, encouraging group members with particular expertise to provide direction.
- Adopting consensus decision making procedures by, for example,

requiring the group to decide criteria for the composition of sub-groups or syndicates.

- Being flexible and open to alternative ideas and views.
- Demonstrating the above by, for example, negotiating content and methods and not strictly adhering to a planned programme.
- Being open and honest with the group.
- Demonstrating the above by practising self-disclosure in terms of, for example, feelings and personal doubts.
- Engaging overall in authentic behaviour in relating to and with the group.

This list is by no means exhaustive. Some behaviours will be more significant in some contexts and may not be relevant at all in others. For example, negotiating content and methods is probably most relevant to maintenance activities than the other contexts described earlier. What is important is that the facilitator occupies a natural leadership position, at least at the beginning of a relationship with a group, and models behaviour which is likely to be emulated by the group. Such behaviour, therefore, must be supportive of establishing and maintaining an appropriate climate.

GIVING AND RECEIVING FEEDBACK

One important reason for having an appropriate climate is to enable relationships to develop which support the giving and receiving of feedback. Feedback itself is critical to facilitating learning and change, especially if the focus is personal attitudes, beliefs and values, and is an essential component of facilitating learning groups.

Problems with feedback

For many individuals giving and receiving feedback is a difficult process. These difficulties can however be overcome with practice and understanding a few simple guidelines. Overall, feedback should be viewed as a gift from one person to another. This emphasizes that feedback is for the benefit of the receiver rather than the giver. It also suggests that the process should be a positive experience for all involved, ie, the giver should derive satisfaction from the benefit gained by the receiver. This is an important point since individuals can experience feelings of guilt in giving negative feedback. If, however, the feedback is given for the right reasons, ie, it is for the benefit of the receiver, then such feelings are not likely to arise.

Negative feedback is often the most difficult to handle. Two thoughts always occur to me when thinking about these difficulties. The first is 'To err is human'. Making or being in error is to be expected of human beings and is not a cause for blame or recrimination. The second is 'We learn from our mistakes'. Receiving feedback on our mistakes is essential if learning is to occur. Indeed, feedback is often essential in recognizing that mistakes have happened. Contributing to the learning of others should be a positive process and it often requires the use of negative feedback.

A final guideline is that openness is essential. Being open has two meanings in the context of feedback. The person giving feedback has to be open about their experience of and feelings about the receiver. Being closed about and hiding such feelings is not likely to be of benefit. The second meaning is being open to feedback as a receiver. Adopting a closed mind to the 'gifts' offered by others will not lead to learning and change.

All of these guidelines need to be adopted by facilitators in their own practice. The behaviour of the facilitator is critical in enabling a learning group to utilize feedback; this means putting into practice the guidelines when relating with a learning group. The giving of feedback by the facilitator and seeking feedback from the group models appropriate behaviour. Doing both well is as important as establishing an appropriate climate in enabling a group to utilize feedback.

Specific guidelines

There are some further more specific guidelines on the use of feedback which should be applied by facilitators and suggested to learning groups:

- Giving feedback   – be honest,
                        be 'other centred',
                        own your feedback,
                        use 'I' statements.
- Receiving feedback – be open,
                        avoid filtering,
                        avoid interpreting.

Detailed guidelines on behaviour are given in Figure 8.4. A useful definition of feedback as it is meant in this context is:

Letting you know how your behaviour affects me and learning from you how my behaviour affects you.

	Helpful	Unhelpful
GIVING	Focus on behaviour	Focus on person
	Based on observation	Based on inference
	Is descriptive	Is judgemental
	Shares information/ideas	Gives advice or direction
	Is specific	Is generalized
	Given immediately	Given after a delay
	Focus on items that can change	Focus on factors outside control of receiver
	Mixes positive and negative	Exclusively positive or negative
RECEIVING	Is receptive	Is defensive
	Listens carefully	Interrupts or challenges
	Acknowledges	Ignores
	Checks understanding	Assumes meanings
	Discusses if required	Refuses to respond

Figure 8.4   *Giving and receiving feedback – guidelines*

INTERVENTION SKILLS

'Intervention skills' refer to a key part of process consultation as described in Chapter 5. Acting as a Process Consultant requires effective intervention skills since the purpose is to enable the client system to identify and solve process problems. This is often achieved by intervening in the process. Deciding when and how to do so is essentially what is meant by intervention skills. However, the same is true of facilitating learning groups since this too involves deciding if, when and how to intervene in the group process. The purpose is also similar because it is to facilitate learning and change. What is written applies equally to process consultation.

Two essential points

It is as well to understand two essential points concerning decisions on intervening in group process:

- The decision belongs to the facilitator alone.
- The decision cannot be reversed.

Both of these may seem obvious but they are important. Facilitators must recognize that they are on their own in making decisions on interventions. The group or individual members cannot be consulted, since to do so would by definition be an intervention in itself. Facilitators must therefore be confident in their judgements. This also applies to the second point. Decisions cannot be reversed and outcomes changed. Facilitators have to be able and willing to live with the consequences of their decisions and actions. My own view is that this offers some comfort to facilitators since it cannot be known what consequences would have followed a different decision or action.

These points are worth illustrating with an example. Suppose a facilitator is working with a task group examining how to implement an organization change in a particular department. Old rivalries between two sections in the department surface at the meeting and focus on two strong personalities from the two sections. The hostility and arguments between these two individuals dominate the discussion and block any real progress. The facilitator faces a first decision of whether to intervene or not. Any reference to other members is in fact a decision to intervene. If the decision is made to intervene the situation may improve or worsen. If it indeed gets worse neither the facilitator nor anyone else can say the intervention was a mistake since it may be that the situation would have worsened even more without the intervention. Facilitators should of course reflect on, analyse and learn from such experiences. They should not however, in my view, indulge in unnecessary guilt and self-recrimination.

Practical guidelines

The example emphasizes two critical issues which should always be taken into account in reaching a decision to intervene:

- Have full knowledge of why.
- Have clear objectives.

The first is particularly important. A situation such as that described in the example can be uncomfortable for all concerned, including the facilitator. It is tempting for the facilitator to intervene in the belief that it is for the benefit of others when in reality it is to cope with the facilitator's own feelings. This temptation should be resisted and facilitators should avoid self-delusion. Other issues to consider are:

- *Needs of the group*
  These are paramount and objectives of interventions should relate to meeting them.

- *Seriousness of the problem*
  The key point here is judging whether or not the group can resolve the problem without help.

- *Motivation*
  Interventions can have positive or negative effects on group motivation and productivity. Obviously the former should be aimed for.

- *Responsibility*
  This should remain with the group. Facilitators should avoid taking it on themselves.

- *Dependency*
  Related to responsibility, dependency, actual or expected, should not be created. Dependency leads to lack of self-respect in the group and is a block to learning.

- *Learning*
  Interventions can be used positively as models or illustrations to help group learning about process issues.

Identifying the need to intervene

All of these factors are of course inter-related and need to be used in combination in judging the use of interventions. They do, however, indicate the important considerations in deciding if and how to intervene. Some useful indicators which can also be used to judge when an intervention is needed are:

- *Destructive behaviour*
  If the group is being destructive of itself and sound relationships.

- *Individual risk*
  Related to the above but here a particular individual is at risk of being hurt or withdrawing from the group.

- *Process issues*
  If the group in general lacks process skills and/or experiences specific process problems, eg, competition for leadership, poor communication.

- *Learning*
  If process issues are impeding learning for individuals and/or the total group.

- *Timing*
  This can be a critical issue though double-edged in application. If problems are experienced early in an activity the judgement may be not to intervene and allow time for the group to resolve the problem. If late in an activity, the judgement may be that it is perhaps too late for resolution. Conversely, early intervention can help prevent later problems and late interventions may be essential to prevent damage.

A classification of interventions

The last item on timing illustrates very clearly that deciding whether to intervene is essentially a matter of judgement. This also applies to decisions on how to intervene. There is a range of possibilities in terms of intervention methods. A classification that I have found personally useful is given in Figure 8.5.

Figure 8.5 illustrates that the approaches vary in intensity as experienced by the learning group. Observation is low intensity while giving direction is high intensity. The continuum also relates to responsibility and dependence which shift to the facilitator as approaches move down the continuum.

Some of the approaches require further comment. Observation refers to simply being present as the group works together. It is, however, an intervention. It will have an effect on the group and 'interfere' with their process. A famous story concerning Chris Argyris illustrates the point.

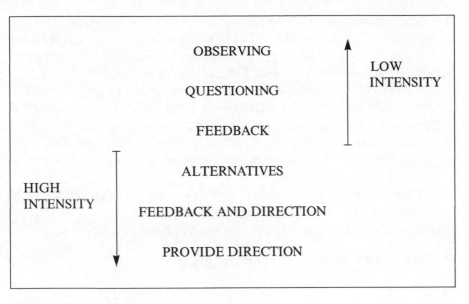

Figure 8.5 *Approaches to interventions*

CASE STUDY 4: THE CHRIS ARGYRIS EXPERIENCE

Many years ago when Argyris was a leading OD consultant specializing in process assignments, he was engaged by a Chief Executive to work with a management team on a strategic review of the company. A day was set aside for the management team to commence the review with Argyris in attendance. After being introduced by the Chief Executive and acknowledging the introductions of the team, Argyris said nothing. Following a short uncomfortable silence during which those present expected Argyris to speak, the Chief Executive proposed an area of discussion and the team began work.

Argyris remained silent throughout the morning session and over lunch. The start of the afternoon session had a shorter and less uncomfortable silence during which, again, Argyris did not speak. The team continued with their work. Around mid-afternoon the Chief Executive was using a flipchart to record some agreed action points. Argyris suddenly rose from his chair and took the pen from the Chief Executive and replaced the cap. He said that the pens dried up if the cap was left off and then sat down. Recovering from their surprise the management team continued and concluded their work by the planned time. The advice on flipchart pens was the only contribution offered by Argyris!

This story illustrates that often the mere presence of a facilitator is all that is required. As Valerie Stewart (1990) says in reporting this story in her book *The David Solution*, Argyris either performed a first class PC service or conducted the greatest 'con' ever. I prefer the former judgement.

Feedback refers to holding up a mirror to the group on their behaviour. It requires being very clear in relation to the process issue concerned. Alternatives mean suggesting a range of options for the group to consider. Again, there is a need to relate to a particular process issue. Direction relates to giving the group clear instructions on behaviours to adopt or actions to take.

Whatever approach is decided on there are a number of guidelines on the way interventions are carried out. Applying these in practice requires flexibility and judgement. My own list is given below:

- Explain the reasons for the intervention.
- Be succinct – do not hog the limelight.
- Start from generalities and move to specifics in the group.
- Live with the consequences – see it through.

SUMMARY

Facilitating learning groups is an essential activity in managing change. Such groups can come together for a variety of reasons in response to organization change, eg, project teams or steering groups; they can be intact work teams; they can come together for overt learning reasons related to a content issue arising from change or maintenance needs. In all cases, effective group processes need to be developed. Facilitating has the dual purpose of enabling that to happen and to enable learning about process.

Ice-breakers, contract setting, trainer behaviour, feedback and intervention skills have been highlighted as essential components of facilitating. Many other skills and techniques could have been chosen, for instance, questioning skills, the use of energizers or interpreting non-verbal behaviour. One critical feature of facilitating not examined is that of learning methods used. These will form part of Chapter 11. Those items addressed in this chapter, especially intervention skills, are considered most relevant to contexts relating to managing change. One of these is team development. This can be a major methodology in OD programmes; it is also the key method of bringing about change in actual work groups. The next chapter, therefore, is devoted to a number of models and theories concerned with team development.

9. Team development

'Team development' is a generic term used to describe a number of approaches to improving the functioning of intact work groups. It is synonymous with 'team building' which has the same purpose. The place of team development as an approach to managing change is now well established. There are two rationales:

1. Effective teams are more open and more flexible and therefore more able to anticipate and respond to change.
2. Effective teams are highly skilled at problem solving and therefore more able to identify and implement appropriate solutions to changed conditions.

In addition, team development is a central focus in organization development. The term can, however, cause confusion since it is often used with different meanings in different contexts, so the starting point in this chapter will be to offer some definitions, which will, in part, explain the theoretical base of team development. This theoretical understanding will be extended by examining the purpose of teams in work organizations. The major content of the chapter will focus on two models I have devised to guide decisions on the use of team development. This will be followed by some examples of team development activities and the chapter will close with a case study on application.

TEAM DEVELOPMENT DEFINED

The use of the word 'team' is itself confusing since it is a noun which is often used as an adjective. As a noun it simply means a collection of individuals who need to work cooperatively to achieve a common objective. A clear example is that of a sports team, with the common objective of securing points or goals in order to win a match. In essence the same is true of work groups. They need to work cooperatively in pursuit of a common objective and therefore can be thought of as teams.

Using 'team' as an adjective

When used as an adjective the word 'team' is normally meant to mean a particular set of characteristics. It is used as a descriptive statement of the condition of the particular group. 'They are a team and we are not' or 'we need to work as a team' are statements often heard in work organizations. What the statements imply is an assessment of the effectiveness of the work group.

Personally I believe this is a misuse of the word. Teams can be effective or ineffective. They are still teams. A soccer team can fail to score goals and lose every match. It is still a team although it is very ineffective. This also applies to work groups in an organization. The word 'team' should, in my view, only be used as a noun to define those groups who need to work cooperatively to achieve a common objective.

Necessary conditions for team development

The last point is in fact critical. A common objective and the requirement for cooperative working to achieve it are essential in defining a team. A team does not and cannot exist if those conditions are absent. This is a useful guide to use in team development work for two reasons. First, it can usefully indicate whether team development is worth pursuing with a particular group. If those conditions are never likely to be true of the group then team development will be wasted effort. However, as we saw in Chapter 7, a total organization could be said by definition to have those characteristics, and therefore they are also true of each and every group within the organization. This gives us our second guide, which is the need to determine the common objectives and build recognition and acceptance of the need to work cooperatively. This is often a useful starting point in team development – which brings us to thinking about the word 'development'.

The meaning of the word 'development'

Development in this context is quite simple. It means the process by which an ineffective team becomes an effective team. The process is of course learning and it involves the team learning about itself and how it can improve. Implicit in this is some notion of effectiveness which the team needs to learn and apply to its own functioning. Effective teams are the same as effective groups, so effective teams have passed through the four stages of group development to 'performing'. They fulfil all of the required task and maintenance functions and exhibit the characteristics of an effective group.

In doing so they also ensure performance of a balanced set of team roles and meet individual needs. Development, then, means a learning process which enables a team to acquire, practise and apply the knowledge and skills required for effective functioning as a group. How such learning can be facilitated will be examined in a later section.

One definition of an effective soccer team is one in which, when the ball floats into the opposing team's goal area, only one player attempts to head it into goal – and that one player is the 'right' one, ie the one who is best at heading goals! This seems to me a perfect illustration of an effective team.

THE ROLE OF TEAMS IN WORK ORGANIZATIONS

The definitions so far indicate that the purpose of team development is to bring about effective functioning with work groups. But why is it that organizations utilize groups in the way they are structured? And why be concerned about the functioning of those groups? The answer to the second question is self-evident though it is in part dealt with in answering the first.

Basically the use of teams reflects two truisms of work organizations:

1. Achievement of individual tasks and goals invariably requires collaboration and cooperation with/from others.
2. Benefits of synergy can be gained from collective action.

Achievement of tasks and goals

The first of these suggests that almost by definition work organizations have to utilize groups. Two examples of what appear to be individual-focused organizational structures reinforce the point. Assembly line manufacturing appears not to be based on teams. However, individual operators are reliant on a range of people in order to carry out their individual tasks, not least the person who precedes them in the line. Others will include those responsible for maintaining tools and machinery used and for supplying materials. The second example is that of a field sales force with individual representatives covering specific geographic territories. Again, each salesperson is dependent on others to achieve their individual task and goals, such as those producing the product or service continuing to meet customer quality and delivery requirements, and also those responsible for the whole range of marketing and promotion activities.

These individual-focused organization structures are often reinforced through HRM policies such as individual performance reward systems based on bonus or commission schemes. This does not alter the reality that individual employees are in fact dependent on cooperative behaviour from others to achieve their individual tasks and are in effect pursuing common objectives. It is possible to argue that the more enlightened and more successful organizations recognize this reality and seek to emphasize the team as opposed to individual focus through organizational structure and policies.

Benefits of synergy

This brings us to the second truism of organizations. Synergy is gained when individuals work cooperatively and collaboratively in teams. The concept is often explained by the equation $2 + 2 = 5$, which simply means that the whole is greater than the sum of the parts. In other words, something extra is created and added to the productivity and quality of work achievable by a group of individuals working as a team. My own favourite analogy of synergy is my liking for toast spread with jam. I like toast by itself and I like jam by itself. Putting them together though creates a third taste which is much nicer and really very different from their separate tastes.

Synergy comes about for a number of reasons. One critical reason is that working in a team is much more satisfying for individuals since human beings are social animals. One illustration of this is the work of Trist and Bamforth (French, 1984; Wilson, 1990) in developing the concept of socio-technical analysis. The basic idea in this concept is that work organizations consist of two inter-related sub-systems: the technical system by which the work is done and the social system which governs the way individuals relate to each other in doing the work. The social system in this sense is the formal part of Herman's 'Iceberg' model discussed in Chapter 4.

CASE STUDY 5: THE SOCIAL SYSTEM AND PRODUCTIVITY

A famous application of socio-technical analysis occurred in the UK coal mining industry. The technical system was changed to accommodate recently developed technology and became what is called the 'long wall' method of mining. However, operating the new machinery and method altered the established team-based working in the mines and therefore also radically changed the existing social system. The effect was that the increase in productivity expected from a more efficient technical system did not materialize; indeed, in many cases productivity worsened. Trist and Bamforth identified the changed social system as the cause and, based on their work, the mining industry adopted new ways of operating the long wall method which accommodated a team-based social system. The results were positive with even greater productivity than originally expected from the technology. The revised operating method required cooperative and collaborative working in pursuit of common objectives and benefits of synergy were gained.

The principles highlighted in this example have been widely applied in practice. In manufacturing, for example, the idea of 'cellular production' which utilizes discrete work teams responsible for discrete products or processes has been found to produce similar results. There are many examples where organization structures and methods of working have recently been changed to accommodate the principles of cellular production. More widely, the trend to divisionalization and the creation of business units or profit centres is growing. Organizations from all sectors of the economy are increasingly looking to devolve accountability and control to the lowest possible level. This helps to sharpen and focus the two conditions necessary for the existence of teams, ie, cooperative working and common objectives, and also enables social systems which support teamworking to operate and evolve. In turn, benefits of synergy are gained, through higher satisfaction from work on the part of individuals. These arguments are of course open to challenge, and the empirical evidence is equivocal (Legge, 1995). However, my own experience supports the conclusion.

A second reason for synergy is the greater spread of knowledge, experience and ideas in teams as opposed to individuals. The collection of ability within individuals is also added to when they work together. An example of this is the use of brain-storming in producing creative ideas. These factors, put together with the greater satisfaction derived from team-based social systems, explain the benefits of matrix organization structures, which are another example of attempts to maximize the benefits of teamwork. Their use also appears to be on the increase, especially in temporary form. The use of project teams and task groups is not confined to dealing with organization change and such groups are now commonly part of the normal methods of carrying out work.

Traditionally such structures have been primarily utilized in organizations or departments subject to continuous environmental change and/or fierce competition, for example research and development and advertising agencies. These examples also have in common the factor of professional or 'knowledge-based' work. As we have already seen, though, the same conditions now apply to all organizations and departments; turbulent environments and constant change are now the norm. Knowledge and the efficient and effective management of information are seen by many as the keys to future success for all organizations. They are also basic requirements of the learning organization, so the use of matrix structures is likely to continue in the future. Their use in industries such as retail, FMCG and financial services are now well established. The trend is continuing and will spread and extend to all parts of the private and public sectors.

Conclusion

We can conclude from this review of the role of teams in organizations that the deliberate and conscious use of teamwork is increasing and is likely to continue to do so in the future. This in turn is leading to an increasing need for effective teams and therefore team development. The number of organizations turning to training practitioners for such services as a means of managing change is ever on the increase. But, where to start? The next section describes a model designed to help answer that question.

A DIAGNOSTIC MODEL

The model identifies two variables as being critical:

1. The setting – who is being developed?
2. The purpose – why does the team exist?

1. The setting

This variable refers to the focus of development. There are two possibilities: either it is the *individual* or it is the *team*. The discussion of the role of teams in organizations demonstrates the need to work cooperatively and collaboratively even when the structure has an individual focus. Membership of overtly recognized teams also requires certain skills on the part of individuals. Therefore, it is often the case that team development requires the development of skills in individuals. In these cases the focus is the *individual* rather than the team.

Each of the two possibilities of individual and team can be further subdivided. Individuals may be being developed separately from their own work group. In this case the Trainer is working with a collection of individuals from a variety of organizations, divisions, departments or sections. The objective will be the development of individual teamwork skills. Alternatively, it is entirely possible to work with an intact work team but still pursue the objective of individual teamwork skills. The objective in both of these settings is to develop individual ability to work as part of a team, ability which the individuals can then bring to any current or future group with which they work.

In the second possibility, that of the team focus, the objective is to identify and address particular problems being experienced by a specific team. There are again two possibilities in terms of setting. The team may be an operational work group consisting of a manager or supervisor with their direct subordinates, eg, a section within a department, or the team may be composed of functional heads responsible jointly and severally for the performance of the whole organization (defined to include subsidiaries, divisions, and departments), eg, a Chief Executive and executive directors forming the management team. The nature and objectives of team development attached to these settings are likely to be very different.

The model is summarized in Figure 9.1. The dotted line indicates that there will be a pay-off for the team in the individual setting and vice versa.

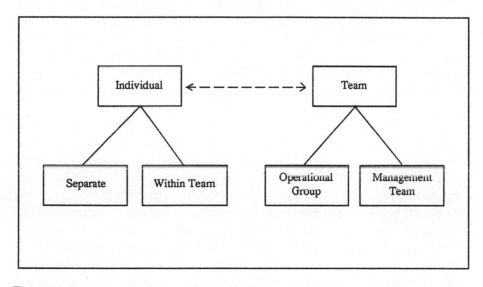

Figure 9.1 *Team development – the possible settings*

2. The purpose

The second key variable is that of purpose. This refers to the purpose of the team in a team setting or the teams from which those being developed in the individual setting are drawn. These purposes should help shape the approach to the development activity. The role of teams in organizations has already been examined in some depth. For this model, however, it is possible to argue that essentially teams exist to solve organizational problems. All organizations have similar problems, for example the setting of objectives, securing and allocating resources, design and control of work, measuring and rewarding performance. However, not all teams have similar organiza-tion problems to solve. To deal with this, the second feature of the model borrows and revises a concept from Revans (1980; 1982) and action learning (see Chapter 11).

Problems can be categorized in two basic forms. The first is the product of specific cause(s) and therefore amenable to treatment by one or at most a few correct solutions. This is defined as a 'puzzle-type' problem. The second form is a situation in which a variety of solutions are available none of which is correct or incorrect. This is defined as a 'decision-type' problem. To illustrate the difference, imagine that the end of year profits in an organization are not known. The 'cause' is that the necessary accounting procedures have not been applied. There is only one correct solution, ie, apply the procedures, and only one 'right' answer, which will be discovered through that process. This is a puzzle-type problem. Once known the amount of profit has to be used. It can be kept in reserves, distributed to shareholders, invested in a variety of ways or perhaps used to fund a pay rise for employees. Making a choice between these possibilities is a decision-type problem.

From this categorization of problems it is possible to conceive a continuum from simple to difficult on which any type of problem can be placed. This allows a more precise definition of the nature and complexity of problems faced by individuals or teams. In turn, this helps in assessing needs and choosing appropriate methods. As a generalization, the lower down the organization hierarchy the more likely it is that the problems will be 'simple' and puzzle-type. There will of course be exceptions, for example the 'shopfloor' staff in social work dealing with the complex human issues involved in a case conference. Those at the highest levels in organizations are more likely to be dealing with problems at the difficult end of the continuum which require decisions rather than identification of cause.

It is useful to divide decision-type problems into sub-categories. There are those which are based on largely factual information and which are made for the most part on rational grounds, eg, whether to invest surplus resources in office automation, new production machinery, vehicles for distribution or a marketing campaign. The second category consists of those decisions about mission, strategy, culture, management style, etc, which are indicative of personal beliefs and values. Such decisions often owe more to emotion than logic (see Stewart, 1994).

This gives us the second part of the model, illustrated in Figure 9.2, which enables an analysis of the nature and complexity of the work of the team to be made.

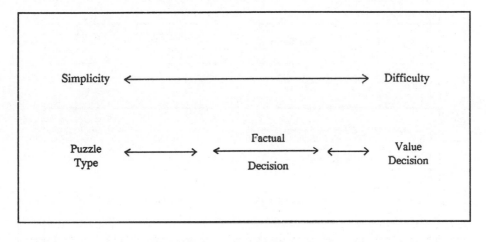

Figure 9.2   *Team development – the possible purposes*

The variables combined

We can now combine the two variables of setting and purpose into the overall model given in Figure 9.3. The two features of the model are shown separately to indicate that they are independent of each other and have no automatic relationship. The utility of the model lies in providing a framework for posing questions which help to diagnose needs prior to designing development activities. Examples of questions which flow from the model are also given in Figure 9.3. Answers are required to both sets of questions before an effective decision on method can be made. A second model which provides a basis for classifying team development methods is described in the next section.

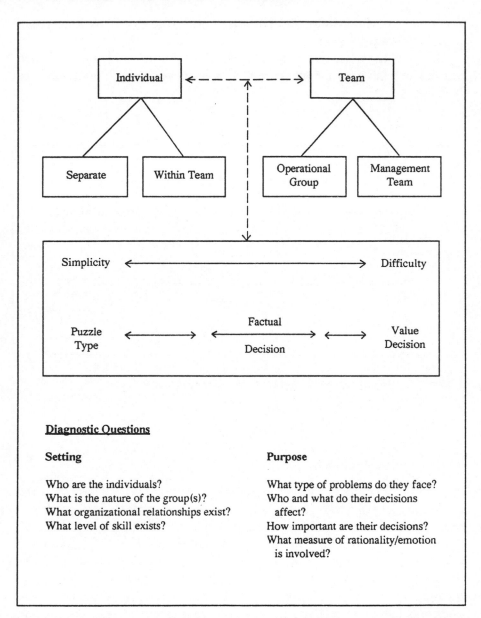

Figure 9.3 *Effective team skills – a diagnostic model*

A CLASSIFICATION MODEL

This model also has two variables.

The variable of issues

The first is to do with issues which need to be addressed in team development work. What I mean by this is the potential causes of dysfunctioning or ineffectiveness within intact work teams. What these causes might be are known from the theories of groups examined in Chapter 7.

In carrying out team development activities there are two broad approaches in terms of this variable. Problems and issues experienced by teams in *general* can be addressed, or the *specific* problems experienced by a particular team can be identified and dealt with. These two possibilities provide the first dimension of the model.

The variable of data focus

The second variable is to do with the source of the data which form the basis of learning in team development. Again there are two possibilities. Data can

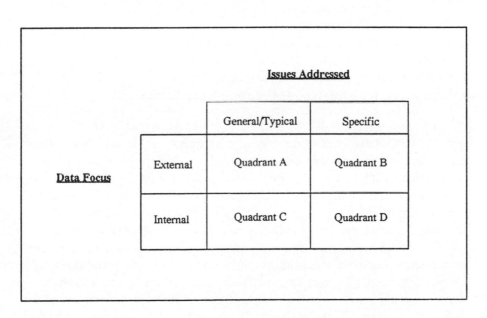

Figure 9.4   *Team development methods – a classification model*

be generated by activities which have an *external* focus or by activities which have an *internal* focus. What is meant here is that externally focused activities involve *simulations* of the kind of work the team carries out. Internally focused activities, in contrast, involve the team carrying out work and tasks associated with their role in the organization.

The two variables of issues and data focus are combined to give four broad categories of team development methods as illustrated in Figure 9.4.

Some common approaches to team development

A number of common approaches to and methods of team development are listed below. Each is allocated to one of the four quadrants in the model to illustrate its application in practice:

	Quadrant
• Unstructured team-based 'T' Group type experiences	D
• Strategic planning workshops	D
• 'Outdoors' development programmes	A
• Team blockage approach	B
• Belbin's team skills management	C
• Use of 'structured experiences', eg, group problem solving exercises	A
• Problem solving and decision making techniques	A
• Semi-structured team-based 'T' Group type experiences	B

This list is obviously not exhaustive or comprehensive. It will also be clear that depending on how a particular method is used it may well fit into more than one quadrant. For example, using outdoors development with an intact work team may well be designed to focus on specific issues of importance to that team. The data, though, will still have an external focus. In those circumstances the method would be classified as Quadrant B.

The value of the model is more as a conceptual tool for practitioners than an academic classification. It allows us to understand with more clarity the use we can make of competing methods, and perhaps more importantly, why we should use one method over another in different circumstances for different purposes. Using the two models together also allows us to identify some general principles.

GENERAL PRINCIPLES OF TEAM SKILLS DEVELOPMENT

There are three important general principles which can be derived from the two models.

1. Individual versus team development needs

The first principle recognizes that effective team functioning requires a certain level of individual skill. A simple example of this is the ability to listen, since high quality listening behaviour is a feature of effective groups. Ineffectiveness in this area is often caused by lack of skill on the part of one or more team members. If this is the case then clearly the development need exists in the individuals rather than the team.

The diagnostic model shows this by highlighting that the development needs will be different in the individual setting to that in the team setting. The classification model gives guidance on appropriate methods. When working in the individual setting, methods which address specific problems will obviously be inappropriate; also, it is not possible to utilize internal data. Therefore, methods from Quadrant A should be utilized. One method identified in Quadrant A is that of structured experiences. The dimension of 'purpose' in the diagnostic model will help determine what type of group problem solving exercises to use, ie, those of a puzzle-type or those requiring group decisions based on personal values.

2. The purpose of the team(s)

Development methods utilized should reflect the purpose for which teams exist. The diagnostic model distinguishes the kind of problems that teams have to solve in organizations.

According to the classification model there are a variety of approaches which can be used in working with intact teams or individuals. Both settings can be accommodated in the model. However, some methods are only appropriate for certain kinds of purpose. For example, using strategy development workshops is only valid when working with members of management teams. While the method can be used for individual or team settings it is likely to be inappropriate for members of operational teams. Conversely, many aspects of problem solving such as situation analysis and cause analysis are only relevant for puzzle-type problems. These are most likely to be dealt with by operational teams, so such methods are most relevant for members of such teams.

3. A natural development path

The third principle is perhaps the most significant and helpful. Our two models and our own experience tell us the following:

- The team setting is the most common for team development activities.
- Activities utilized in this setting must at some point arrive at those in Quadrant D of Figure 9.4.

However, it is also generally the case that team development activities vary in their ease of use from the point of view of both the practitioner and team members. Discussing general issues to do with the functioning of teams is easier for both since this tends to happen at an intellectual level. Once the focus is on specific issues to do with a particular team then discussion becomes more personal and therefore more emotional. Similarly with the complexity of data. Data which have an external focus are generally less complex than those which have an internal focus. The latter tends to have a history behind it which has often not been overtly identified or brought into

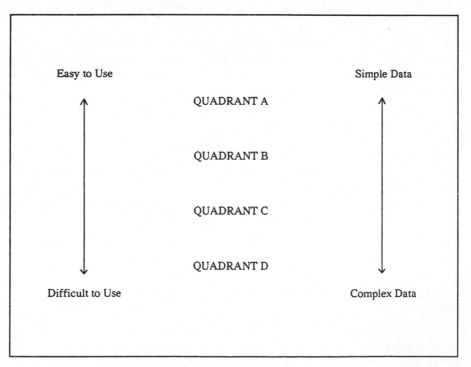

Figure 9.5 *A continuum of methods*

the open by the team. A great deal more analysis and discussion is required before the data become meaningful to the team and useful in development terms.

These two points are of course generalizations but they do suggest a general principle which is true of team development methods – that methods increase in difficulty to utilize and in the complexity of data generated as we move through the classification model. This principle is illustrated in Figure 9.5.

To the extent that this principle holds true we can identify a natural development path, illustrated in Figure 9.6, which is to start with that which is easy to use and which utilizes simple data. As the team grows in experience and confidence in examining team-related issues, and mutual trust builds between them and the practitioner, then activities can start to focus on the difficult and complex end of the continuum. My own experience of facilitating team development programmes with intact teams confirms that this is a useful path to follow, and that the principle holds true irrespective of the team setting or the team purpose identified in Figure 9.3. The nature of the activities will vary according to those two variables but the development path remains the same.

SOME TEAM DEVELOPMENT ACTIVITIES

HRM and HRD specialists are the obvious and natural providers of team development services in organizations. In providing such services practitioners need to apply the skills associated with Process Consultation and facilitating already described. Often team development with intact work groups requires the practitioner to solely adopt a PC role. This is especially the case in Quadrant D in the management team settings. Whatever the setting and purpose, however, and whatever Quadrant methods are selected from, the primary role is always that of facilitator rather than instructor. Team skills and team development cannot be achieved through traditional direct training.

Within that context the purpose of this section is to provide a limited number of examples of the kind of activities that can be used in team development work. The examples will hopefully provide a flavour of team development in practice and will also further illustrate the meaning and use of the models described in this chapter. The bibliography does of course include some sources which provide an extensive range of activities.

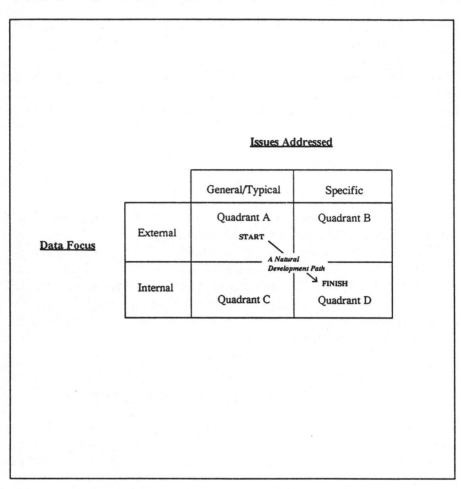

Figure 9.6 *A natural development path*

Exploring individual needs

The first set of activities is designed to illustrate and explore the needs of individuals in relation to their membership of teams. These were identified in Chapter 7 as the needs of *inclusion*, *control* and *affection*. The activities can be utilized for any combination of the variables identified in the diagnostic model. In terms of the individual setting the objective of the activities will relate to learning about theory. When used in a team setting the activities can be useful for diagnostic purposes when attempting to identify team-specific issues. Figure 9.7 describes these activities.

1. <u>**Control**</u>

    a) - Request individuals to stand in a circle around a table on which there is a large sheet of paper (Flipchart paper is ideal).
        - Explain that the paper represents power and control in the team and that when you 'give the word' all team members should lift the paper.
        - Give the word.
        - Discuss and process the results.

    b) - Divide team members into pairs with one partner sitting on a chair and the other sitting on the floor facing the seated person.
        - Explain that the person on the floor has to get their seated partner to swap places with them.
        - When all have swapped repeat the instruction.
        - Discuss and process the results.

    c) - Request team members to form a line representing the order of power and influence in the team.
        - Discuss and process the results.

2. <u>**Inclusion**</u>

    a) - Request team members to form a standing circle which is closed by having members' arms around each others' waist.
        - Instruct one member to stay outside of the circle and then attempt to gain entry.
        - Repeat with each team member.
        - Discuss and process the results.

    b) - Designate a spot in the room.
        - Instruct the team that all members who feel part of the team should occupy that spot.
        - Discuss and process the results.

3. <u>**Affection**</u>

        - Request team members to sit in a circle facing each other.
        - Instruct one team member to face each other member in turn and complete the statement 'What I like about you ...'.
        - Repeat with all other team members.
        - Discuss and process results.

Figure 9.7   *Activities for exploring individual needs*

It will be clear from Figure 9.7 that the activities are only workable in the individual setting when the learning group has had time to become established.

Instructions: Below is a list of statements describing possible contributions to effective teams. Score each statement according to the following scale:

1 = Not very often true of me
2 = Sometimes true of me
3 = Very often true of me

Score

(1) I express my opinion concerning our work and tasks ———

(2) I suggest ways of tackling work problems ———

(3) I comment on the way the team works together ———

(4) I propose that other views within the team are sought ———

(5) I ask other people for their views on work problems ———

(6) I summarize progress at various stages of discussion on work problems ———

(7) I listen when other people are speaking in team meetings ———

(8) I offer humorous comments to bring 'light relief' ———

(9) I make suggestions as to who should do what ———

(10) I comment on the suggestions of others ———

(11) I ask questions to help clarify understanding for myself and/or others ———

(12) I try to resolve disagreements between other members ———

(13) I spot and analyse weaknesses in the way we carry out our work ———

(14) I act as a link between other members in relation to work tasks ———

(15) I comment on the way team members observe standards of behaviour ———

(16) I do not engage in separate conversations during team meetings ———

Scoring Sheet

Instructions: Transfer your scores from the analysis sheet to the table below:

Task-Related Behaviours	Maintenance-Related Behaviours
Statement 1 2 5 6 9 10 13 14 ——— TOTAL ———	Statement 3 4 7 8 11 12 15 16 ——— TOTAL ———

Figure 9.8   *Effective teamwork – a self-analysis instrument*

Exploring group functions

A further activity which is also of use in both team and individual settings is given in Figure 9.8. It is an instrument designed to explore the group functions identified in Chapter 7. I originally devised the instrument for use with intact work teams and have used it with both operational and management teams. However, more recently I have used it in individual settings to aid learning about theory. It can of course have that purpose in team settings. The purpose in those circumstances is also diagnostic and action-oriented in terms of dealing with team-specific issues. The instrument enables a team to identify what functions are not being performed adequately and why. It also enables agreement to be reached on actions to be taken by individual members to ensure those missing functions are performed in the future.

The instrument is by no means scientifically rigorous, but it is useful for generating data which can then be further analysed and explored. The actual results are often less important than the resulting interpretation.

A comparison with Belbin

Utilizing the instrument is in some ways similar to the approach generally adopted in using Belbin's model of team roles (Belbin, 1981). There is a more rigorously tested self-assessment instrument available in Belbin's book which enables individuals to identify their preferred team role(s) and a given team their existing balance of roles. I have found that both instruments and models have similar results, ie, the use of the subsequent data is more critical than the data themselves. For this reason I do not favour one model or instrument over the other; indeed, I have often used both with intact work teams as complementary frameworks for diagnosing and solving team-specific problems. I also commonly use both in individual settings when developing teamwork skills. There is one point I would make in commenting on Belbin's work, which is that I do not see his model as exclusively applying to management teams. In my experience operational teams can also gain a lot of development from utilizing the model.

Exploring team dysfunctioning

The third activity I want to describe is solely for use in team settings. Its purpose is both diagnostic and developmental and the focus is definitely within Quadrant D of Figure 9.4. As with the instruments just discussed, the critical part of the activity is in interpreting and using the data generated as a basis for action decisions. It is during this stage that the practitioner's facilitating skills are critical, especially in terms of feedback and interventions. The activity is also an interesting example of the Survey Feedback method in OD described in Chapter 5. The basic steps are given in Figure 9.9.

This activity is not recommended as an initial start point in team development unless sound relationships already exist within the team and with the practitioner. It should also be clear that an appropriate contract needs to be entered into by all team members before using the activity. The duration of the activity is obviously a critical issue but is very difficult to predict. Personally I would expect a minimum of one full day to complete all stages but it may of course take much longer. The actual time taken can be spread over a longer time period depending on how the team development programme is structured.

Stage1

a)   Request team members to write on one piece of paper one reason why they enjoy being a member of the team and one reason why they do not.

b)   Collect and shuffle the pieces of paper and re-distribute them randomly among team members.

c)   Request team members to read out in turn what is written on the paper given to them and put these on a flipchart under the headings of DO ENJOY/DON'T ENJOY.

d)   Team members discuss the results and agree a definitive list.

Stage 2

a)   Request team members to write on one piece of paper one strength and one weakness in the way the team works together.

b)   Repeat steps b to d of Stage 1.

Stage 3

a)   Request team members to discuss and agree the following:

     1)   Action to be taken to improve team functioning.
     2)   Behaviours expected of all team members to improve team functioning.
     3)   Methods and procedures for monitoring implementation of 1) and 2).

NB   Depending on the number of team members, Stage 3 can be given as a sub-group task with the conclusions of each sub-group discussed and agreed by the whole team in a plenary session.

Figure 9.9   *Team development – a diagnostic/development activity*

TEAM DEVELOPMENT IN ACTION

I will close this chapter with a short case study.

CASE STUDY 6: TEAM DEVELOPMENT IN ACTION

The situation

The case involves a management team of a large department in a public authority. The organization as a whole was subject to major environmental change. Much of this emanated from national legislation, but many other changes happening in society generally were also having an impact. The common factor in these changes was a drive to more 'customer-oriented' services being provided by the authority. A new chief executive had been appointed to the organization, partly in response to these external pressures; this had the effect of adding an internal source of change.

The head of the department was concerned that he and his management team were not really getting to grips with this changing situation. The team was long-established with no major changes in composition for over six years. Their ways of working were also well-established but had evolved in more stable times. A further concern of the department head was that, as a member of the organization's management team, he was expected by the new chief executive to set an example to other senior managers in the way he led his department.

The diagnosis

It was against this background that I was asked to provide help in terms of team development. It was during an initial interview with the manager (I will use that term from this point as it is shorter than head of department) that these points emerged. I requested and received agreement that I conduct interviews with individual members of the management team.

This initial diagnostic activity confirmed the manager's assessment of the need for team development. It also revealed support for the idea from all team members which was of course critical. Using the diagnostic model I was able to determine that the setting was primarily management team although individual skill development was also a need; this, though, could be addressed within the team. The purpose of the team lay in the difficult area involving both factual and value-based decisions.

The design

Based on this diagnostic activity I designed a two-stage development pro-gramme. The starting point was a two-day strategy development workshop which constituted Stage 1. This included a mixture of activities but focused on Quadrant

D in the classification model. The decision on focus was taken in the knowledge of existing sound relationships within the team and the high degree of support for a development activity. My proposed role in the workshop was primarily that of facilitator and process consultant. This last role was to continue in Stage 2. This involved a continuation of my involvement by attending a minimum of three team meetings following the workshop. A need for continued involvement would be

Day One

9.30 - 9.45	Introduction and Scene Setting
9.45 - 10.30	Contract Setting
10.30 - 11.30	XYZ Organization - The Future
11.30 - 12.30	Managing Change
12.30 - 2.30	Current Changes - Lessons Learned
2.30 - 3.30	Effective Teams - A Model
3.30 - 4.30	Review of Team Working
4.30 - 5.30	Analysing Organizations - A Model
7.30 - 9.30	ABC Department in XYZ Organization

Day Two

9.00 - 10.30	Analysing Organizations - A Second Model
10.30 - 12.00	Effective Teams - A Second Model
12.00 - 3.30	Agenda Setting and Action Plans
3.30 - 4.00	Initial Report Back to CE
4.00 - 4.30	Closing Exercise and Review

Figure 9.10   *Strategy development workshop programme*

reviewed at the third meeting. I presented these ideas to a team meeting where the programme was discussed and agreed by all team members. The programme for the strategy development workshop is given in Figure 9.10.

A number of explanatory points are required to understand the operation of the programme.

All timings were flexible and breaks were taken as and when appropriate.

I had suggested informing and involving the new Chief Executive in the activity since the manager was concerned to build a relationship. The outcome was a one-hour presentation by the Chief Executive on the future of the organization and his attendance for a verbal report on the initial outcomes. He did not attend any other parts of the workshop.

Related to these outcomes, a major focus was on strategic planning for the department. Pre-work was utilized in the form of a STEP and a SWOT analysis being prepared by each team member. These were discussed and analysed at the workshop during what were in effect normally conducted team meetings. The results formed a major part of the Agenda Setting and Action Planning session.

Two models of effective groups, ie, Tuckman's stages of group development and the features of effective groups described in Chapter 7, were introduced to the team during the workshop. These models were immediately applied to the team itself by individual members rating the team according to the models. For instance, the 'Features of Effective Groups' were each given a score of between 1 and 5 by each member according to how they saw their team's performance. These were then collated and discussed by the team. The results of these discussions formed the other major part of the Agenda Setting and Action Planning session.

When the team members were discussing and formulating strategic plans for their department and during the sessions when they were analysing their functioning as a team, my own role was that of process consultant. This was also my role during the Agenda Setting and Action Planning session.

The outcomes

The workshop ended with the team having a clearer and, more importantly, a shared vision of their department's future. Associated with this was an agreed action plan covering the weeks and months ahead. They also had as part of their action plan, agreement on changes in the way they worked together. This included, for example, focusing on one critical strategic issue at each meeting and sharing the chairing of team meetings according to who had lead responsibility for the issue under discussion. An additional item was to review team working on a regular basis. This is not to say that such procedures are universally applicable but that *this* team believed they would improve its functioning.

I continued in the role of process consultant for the planned three meetings.

The team itself reviewed its functioning at the end of the third meeting and my involvement ceased by mutual agreement. My own assessment was that this particular team had benefited from its overt development and were at least much more confident in their ability to manage the many changes facing them. I heard from the manager about six months after the end of the programme who contacted me to say things were going well and the team was still learning!

SUMMARY

We have seen in this chapter that team development is concerned with improving the functioning of work groups in terms of utilizing cooperative behaviours in pursuit of common objectives. This improvement can focus on individuals as well as intact teams and essentially involves development experiences utilizing a variety of approaches and methods. The available approaches and methods can be categorized according to the two variables of data focus and issues addressed.

The chapter has emphasized the role of individual learning in managing organization change. Teams and organizations depend on individuals learning new knowledge, skills and attitudes in order to bring about change. The following chapters focus on the critical issue of individual change.

10. Theories of learning and attitude change

Training and development is essentially concerned with achieving individual change through learning. Change within organizations requires such learning to occur. It is therefore critical for training practitioners to have and apply a sound understanding of individual learning if they are to effectively contribute to managing organization change. However, we know from a study of OD that the focus of learning cannot be confined to knowledge and skills. Individual beliefs, values and attitudes play an important part in creating a learning organization and in successful implementation of planned organization change. Training specialists also need a sound understanding of change processes in these areas.

This chapter focuses on some relevant theories in achieving individual change. One set of theories relate to the learning process and how change through learning can be promoted. The second set of ideas are to do with the role of attitudes and how they can be influenced. Both sets of theories underpin many approaches to training and development currently in use and which are particularly relevant when thinking about managing organization change. Approaches that I have found most effective and which I believe to be most relevant to organization change are described in the next chapter. This chapter begins with some basic ideas which themselves provide the basis for the theories examined in later sections.

THE THREE LEVELS OF EXISTENCE

As individual human beings we experience our lives at three levels of existence. In simple terms they can be described by the phrase 'we think, we feel, we do'.

The relationship between the levels

All three levels are inter-related and interactive. This means that what we think is influenced by and in turn influences what we feel and do; the same is true of each level in relation to the other two. For example what we do is influenced by and in turn influences what we think and what we feel. In the language of psychology these three levels are termed the cognitive domain, the affective domain and the action domain.

It is also true that we experience our existence at all three levels simultaneously and therefore cannot really disassociate one level from another. For instance, as you read these words you are doing, ie, you are experiencing the action domain. This is because perception is an active process, physiologically and psychologically, which needs to be engaged in order to read. Reading is also a thinking process and therefore you are engaged in the cognitive domain. Finally, what you are reading and your thoughts concerning it have relationships with your existing beliefs about and attitudes towards the subject. Therefore your feelings are involved and you are also in the affective domain.

You are unlikely to be conscious of your experience of the affective domain in reading these words unless they explicitly contradict or actively re-affirm your current beliefs and related attitudes. Similarly, you will not be conscious of the action domain in consciously attempting to focus your eyes. At a conscious level you are only aware of the cognitive domain, ie, your thinking process. This does not mean that your experience of reading these words is confined to that level. Human existence is experienced at all three levels.

The three levels and learning

If that last statement is accepted, it follows that learning is experienced at all three levels. Since cognition, affection and action occur simultaneously, learning both influences and is influenced by all three domains. What you learn from this book will be the result of the interaction between the three domains as you read it. Any theory of learning therefore has to be able to explain the process in terms of the three levels of existence, and it has to be applicable in promoting learning through utilizing the cognitive, affective and action domains. These two points underpin important theories of learning.

THE QUESTION OF BEHAVIOUR

Before examining theories of learning we need to address the issue of behaviour. There are two critical problems associated with the concept. The first is one of definition and the second is to do with cause.

Defining behaviour

Peter Honey, a leading occupational psychologist and training consultant, offers a simple definition of behaviour (Honey, 1988) – he suggests that behaviour is everything we say and everything we do. There is an implicit relationship in this definition between the concept of behaviour and the action domain. Behaviour is about doing. It is what can be observed and measured. The cognitive and affective domains are difficult if not impossible to observe and they present great problems in measurement. There are of course means of measuring attitudes, part of the affective domain, through survey instruments, but the instruments and the results achieved are open to challenge. We cannot therefore easily access the cognitive and affective domains of people in general. (We often have trouble enough accessing our own! For example, what do you really *think* and *feel* about your organization?) Because of this many psychologists consider behaviour as the only worthwhile focus of study.

There are problems with the definition. I have already said that physical perception through the sense organs is an active process and part of the action domain. Some elements of perception can be observed and measured fairly easily, for example the extent of and changes in dilation of the pupil in the eye. The actions of other sense organs though, for example the ear, do not lend themselves so easily to observation and measurement.

Another problem is distinguishing exactly what constitutes 'doing'. If doing equates with action and action equates with behaviour and behaviour equates with what is observable and measurable then it must be the case that when we are thinking we are doing nothing! Since the thinking process is not observable or measurable it is excluded from behaviour and therefore is not part of 'doing'. This seems to me nonsensical and inconsistent with everyone's personal experience. Sitting in a chair perfectly still perhaps with my eyes closed and displaying no observable behaviour does not mean I am doing nothing. What I am doing is thinking.

Some psychologists in defining the focus on and definition of behaviour may point to observable eye movements beneath my eyelids as the only valid evidence that I am in fact thinking. In doing so they would also, although not necessarily intentionally, be confirming my earlier point that we experience the three levels of existence simultaneously. More critically, they would be illustrating the importance of behaviour and the action domain as an indicator of the existence of the cognitive and affective domains, and any changes within them. For instance, my actions reflect and enable inferences to be drawn about the current condition of my feelings towards my job and my employing organization. If I regularly turn up on time and leave on time it may be a reasonable inference that I have a positive attitude. If I begin to arrive late and leave early it is reasonable to infer that my attitude may have changed. Which brings us to the problem of cause.

The cause of behaviour

What exactly causes behaviour? Is it the cognitive domain or the affective domain or both? There are of course many theories which seek to explain the cause of human behaviour. Those which focus on the concept of 'motivation' are perhaps most well known in explaining the phenomenon. Some of these focus on the existence of genetically determined inherent drives which form part of the 'natural' human psyche and which are shared by all individuals. Alternative theories reject the notion of inherent drives and postulate that all behaviour is the result of individual experience. In these cases the suggestion is that all behaviour is 'learned', and therefore can be changed through the same process. How that process works is the subject of debate within that school of thought. Ideas put forward include classical conditioning, operant conditioning, imitation and identification depending on whether the original source is Pavlov, Skinner or Bandura (Bandura, 1977; Ribeaux, 1978).

There is room for debate on the causal chain between, for instance, attitudes and behaviour. What is clear though from current theory and research is that there is a direct relationship between learning and behaviour. It is probably also the case that the relationship operates in both directions; that is that behaviour is at least partly the result of learning and that learning is at least in part the result of behaviour. It follows from this that learning is an important means of changing behaviour and that the process of learning needs to engage learners in behaving, ie, doing. Since human beings experience the three levels of existence simultaneously this will also engage learners in the cognitive and affective domains. So what appears to be required is a theory of learning which applies these principles in practice. There are in fact two such theories which have many similarities and which are now commonly utilized in training and development.

SYSTEM BETA

Reg Revans is the originator of an approach to management development called 'Action Learning', which is examined in the next chapter. One of the key assumptions which underpins Action Learning is a theory of how individuals learn. Revans labelled his theory System Beta (Revans, 1980; 1982).

The basic idea of System Beta is that the learning process closely approximates what is known as the 'Scientific Method'. This latter concept is to do with the rules and processes which govern scientific enquiry and investigation. In practice it is postulated as the way in which all new knowledge and understanding is gained. It seems therefore a reasonable suggestion that similar processes operate in individuals in terms of learning.

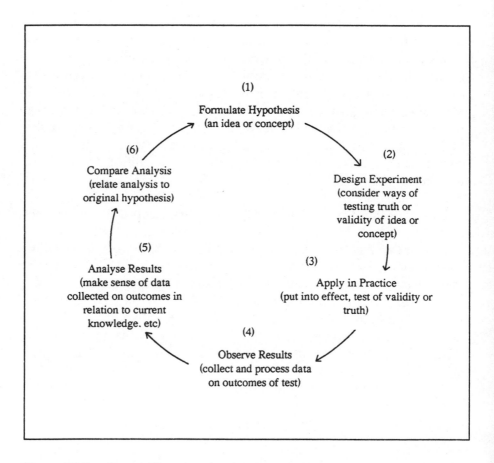

Figure 10.1 *System Beta*

Stages involved in System Beta

System Beta suggests four key stages in the learning process based on the Scientific Method.

1. Formulate hypothesis.
2. Design experiment.
3. Apply experiment, observe and analyse results.
4. Accept, reject or re-frame hypothesis.

These four stages are in fact cyclical and continuous in individual learning. Each of them also encompasses further activities within the total cycle. A fuller exposition of the process is given in Figure 10.1.

It will be clear from Figure 10.1 that System Beta engages an individual learner in all three levels of existence. The process described involves the cognitive, affective and action domains. Revans suggests that all human learning at the individual level occurs through this process.

Two critical features

A critical feature of the process is the starting point of the hypothesis. The idea or concept in this stage is formulated by and belongs to the individual. This means two possibilities in practice. The first is that it may be an original and unique idea that is formulated by the individual. The second is that the idea or concept is presented to the individual by someone else through, for example, a lecture, a book or a conversation. According to the model, however, the individual in both cases will need to complete all stages of the cycle in order for the learning to occur. In the latter case doing so will also probably have the effect of producing an individual interpretation of the concept, therefore each individual's learning remains unique. It also follows that in the case of a presented concept through, for example, a lecture, learning does not happen unless and until all stages of the process are completed. This point is obviously significant in the design of learning opportunities within training and development.

A second significant feature of the model is that because the process is cyclical the starting point does not have to be the formulation of the hypothesis. Individuals can and do enter the cycle at different points in relation to separate pieces of learning. The stages in Figure 10.1 are labelled with numbers in sequence for convenience rather than to represent reality. For instance, it is common for new ideas or concepts to suggest themselves in stages three, four and five.

System Beta examined

System Beta makes sense to me in terms of explaining my personal experience of learning and the observations I have made of the learning of others. There are, of course, alternative theories of the learning process. These generally fall into one of two classifications either behaviourist or cognitive. I do not intend to describe all of the theories here since I am focusing on two I consider most relevant to managing change. However, I would suggest that there are no insurmountable contradictions between System Beta and theories belonging to the behaviourist and cognitive schools of thought. I would further suggest that System Beta is a comprehensive and cohesive theory which is capable of encompassing alternatives. These two suggestions also apply to the second theory of learning that I describe in the next section and which has many similarities with System Beta.

EXPERIENTIAL LEARNING

The theory known as 'experiential learning' was developed by the American psychologist David Kolb and his co-workers in the mid-1970s (Kolb et al, 1984). Since then it has become one of the most well known and widely applied theories in training and development, especially in terms of managing organization change and in related adult learning. The theory is very similar to System Beta.

Rationale of experiential learning

The rationale of experiential learning is quite simple. It is that learning approximates the process of problem solving, and that therefore teaching or training which is designed to encourage, support and enable learning should be based on a problem solving approach. This basic idea is worth exploring in a little more detail.

Traditional teaching methods are based on ideas which have particular associations. These associations include:

- the presence of and key role for a teacher or trainer;
- a particular and specific place for learning to occur such as a classroom or training centre;
- a focus on knowledge, ideas and concepts; and
- the use of learning materials such as textbooks and handouts.

Such associations produce particular meanings that are attached to the learning process. These include the meaning that:

- an individual's learning is the responsibility of some other person, eg, the teacher;
- that learning is a separate and discrete activity that occurs at particular times in a specific place;
- that learning is essentially a passive process; and
- that learning is concerned with acquiring or understanding abstract information, ideas and concepts.

It can be argued with great justification that most individuals' experience of formal learning leads to these associations and produces these meanings.

An alternative is to view learning as similar to problem solving. In this case the associations are that:

- problems are very specific;
- they belong to the individual and are their responsibility to solve; and
- that they require experimentation as part of the process of reaching a solution.

These associations produce a different set of meanings:

- problem solving is an active process;
- it is concerned with practical application and results;
- the focus is real and concrete; and
- problem solving is a continuous and natural part of living.

What this means in practice is that most individuals actually learn passivity and dependence in relation to learning through their experience of traditional methods. It also means that traditional methods do not actually reflect the reality of learning since they do not adopt a problem solving approach. Using problem solving as a basis for explaining the learning process leads to the theory of experiential learning. This is represented in Figure 10.2.

Features of experiential learning

The process described in Figure 10.2 is, according to Kolb, how people actually learn. As with System Beta all stages need to be completed in order

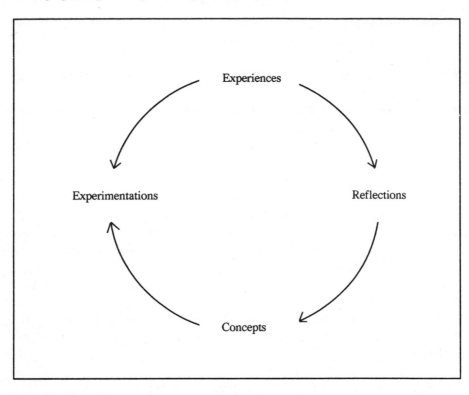

Figure 10.2   *Based on Kolb's experiential learning cycle*
(Source: Kolb et al, 1984.*)*

for learning to occur and the cycle can be entered at any stage. The cycle is also continuously occurring and re-occurring within individuals in relation to a multitude of learning foci. The focus of learning is however goal-driven. This means that the direction of individual learning, ie, *what* is being learned, is governed by felt needs experienced and/or objectives being pursued by the particular individual.

The last point is significant in underpinning a further important feature of experiential learning. Since learning is individually goal-driven there will be variations in emphasis on the different stages of the process because the nature of learning goals will vary. For instance, a manager may be very concerned with practical application and so is more interested in active experimentation and concrete experiences. Conversely, a theoretical scientist may be more concerned with formulating general principles or laws and therefore is more interested in reflecting on observations in order to produce abstract concepts and generalizations. These two individuals will pay greater attention to the stages of the process which seem most relevant to their particular learning needs and goals. This leads to the idea of learning styles which suggests that each individual has a preferred approach to learning represented by their learning style.

The four learning styles identified by Kolb

Kolb suggests four broad learning styles based on the experiential learning cycle. Each style is the result of a different combination of two stages in the cycle.

- *The Diverger*
  This style combines an emphasis on concrete experiences and reflective observation. This involves actually carrying out tasks and then thinking about the process adopted and results achieved.

- *The Assimilator*
  This style combines reflective observation and abstract conceptualization. It involves using data and analysis in reflective observation to generalize and produce sound theories and models for wider application.

- *The Converger*
  Combines abstract conceptualization and active experimentation. This style concentrates on application and testing of theories and general principles to specific problems and situations.

- *The Accommodator*
  Combines active experimentation and concrete experiences. This is an action-oriented style which does not place great value on cognitive processes, and focuses most on actually experiencing and producing workable results.

The idea of learning styles is important. The experiential learning cycle, in common with System Beta, tells us that a number of stages need to happen for learning to occur. However, if different individuals have different learning styles they may miss out on learning opportunities by emphasizing only some stages at the expense of others. If the cycle is valid as a theory then it is the case that individuals have to engage in all four stages before they have actually learned effectively; it is a critical requirement that *all* learners engage in *all* stages of the cycle.

This has led to one application of the learning cycle being in the area of *learning to learn*. This obviously has great relevance in managing organization change since, as we saw in Chapter 6, a learning organization depends on effective individual learners. A refinement of Kolb's theory as it relates to learning styles is of practical help in producing effective learners and in improving organizational learning. The refinement was developed by two British researchers, Honey and Mumford, who have now produced numerous books on their ideas on learning styles (Honey and Mumford, 1986; 1989).

Learning styles identified by Honey and Mumford

The Honey and Mumford model accepts the experiential learning cycle and the basic idea of four learning styles. However, the model concentrates on

1.	ACTIVIST	-	Emphasizes the concrete experience stage of the cycle. Enjoys and learns best from new experiences in the 'here and now'. Corresponds most closely with Kolb's Diverger.
2.	REFLECTOR	-	Focuses on the reflective observation stage of the cycle. Individuals with this style tend to stand back from direct experience and instead undertake a thorough collection and analysis of data. Matches most closely the Assimilator.
3.	THEORIST	-	This style is related to the abstract conceptualization stage of the cycle. The emphasis is on making sense of data in a logical way and to produce a synthesis which holds true in a wide range of applications. Equates with the Converger.
4.	PRAGMATIST	-	Individuals with this style focus on the active experimentation stage of the cycle. Their concern is with trying things out in practice and establishing what works. Practical application and results are important rather than an understanding of how and why. Corresponds to the Accommodator style.

Figure 10.3 *The four styles of Honey and Mumford*

only one stage of the cycle as being related to a particular style, in contrast to Kolb who holds that each style is the result of two stages in combination. This leads Honey and Mumford to offer different names to their four styles. What these are and how they correspond to the ideas of Kolb is described in Figure 10.3.

APPLYING THEORY IN PRACTICE

There are a number of significant conclusions that can be drawn from these theories of learning that are important for the practice of training and development. The most critical are discussed below.

Learning is continuous

What this means in practice is that individuals are learning all the time and not just when they are being educated or trained. If the theories described here are valid then work, home and social activities and experiences are just as important in development as more formal or traditional training activities such as courses. This has two important implications. First, formal training activities should not ignore the realities of other learning contexts. An example of this in practice is the 'holistic' approach to management development which views participants as whole individuals rather than simply 'managers', and as people who need to manage their development in terms of home and social settings as well as in the work context. The second implication is that training and development can and should utilize methods which manage the learning process outside of formal settings.

Learning is goal- or need-directed

This means that individuals direct their learning to satisfy their own needs and meet their personal goals and objectives. What follows from this is that the focus, subject or content of training and development must be seen as relevant by learners in their own terms. For instance, you will not learn anything from reading this book unless its content contains items relevant to you. However, the fact that you have decided to read the book suggests that this is likely to be the case. The general point remains, though, that training and development is only likely to be effective to the extent that it relates to real needs and personally relevant objectives.

Learning requires engagement in separate but related activities

Both System Beta and experiential learning emphasize that the learning process consists of a number of stages which must happen for learning to occur. Applying this in practice means that the design of training and development must enable each of these stages to be engaged. The experiential learning cycle provides a useful model to follow in designing training and development activities. If it is used then by definition the learning cycle is complete and effective learning is *possible*. The next conclusion explains why it is not possible for us to say that learning will always occur.

Individuals have different learning styles

This conclusion does not mean that every individual has a different style unique to themselves. Nor does it mean that every individual has only one style. It does, however, mean that every individual will have a preferred or dominant learning style within the categories identified by Kolb and by Honey and Mumford. Using the learning cycle as a basis for design means that all styles are catered for, so that not only is the learning cycle completed but also the learning experience contains activities which are suited to all styles. However, if a particular individual has a very dominant style which excludes engagement in activities related to other styles and therefore other stages of the cycle, that person will not learn effectively. This will be true throughout all aspects of the person's life including experiences of training and development, however well designed and delivered. In my view such an individual will be rare but, according to the theory, can exist.

Learning is an ability which can be developed and improved

Such individuals can be helped. Both Kolb et al and Honey and Mumford have produced instruments which enable preferred learning styles to be identified. The latter have utilized extensive research to develop an 80-item questionnaire based on a simple choice of agree/disagree to each item. Using the questionnaire as a basis, the researchers have devised a series of activities and lists of advice designed to improve weak areas. For instance, if an individual produces a score indicating a low or very low preference for the Reflector style (the ratings of raw scores are based on norms as with standard psychometric instruments) then some of the advice provided to develop that style is as given in the following list:

- Practise observing behaviour at meetings.
- Keep a diary and read/reflect on content at weekends.
- Based on the above, reach conclusions about own behaviour.

- Write a short review of each meeting attended.
- Carry out research into a work-related topic.
- Select a controversial topic, eg, capital punishment, and produce a paper examining the pros and cons.

The above is a single and brief example. Honey and Mumford's publications help individuals learn how to learn by improving and developing weak styles. Some of their publications also help to focus on organizational learning in terms of building in and maximizing learning opportunities as part of organization functioning and operations.

The implication of this conclusion is that there is a role for training and development in developing learning ability in both individuals and organizations. One constraint in applying this and many other conclusions from this chapter so far is that of *attitudes* towards learning. As indicated at the beginning of the chapter, attitude formation and change is critical not only to learning but also to organization change in general. The next section examines this important subject.

ATTITUDE FORMATION AND CHANGE

The study of attitudes has concerned psychologists, sociologists and social psychologists for many years. Some of the earliest studies date back to the beginning of this century and as we approach the start of the next many of the same questions remain unanswered.

Attitude and behaviour

A current example in the UK is the implementation of equal opportunities policies. Over the last 20 or so years awareness-raising programmes on issues such as sexism, racism and discrimination against people with disabilities have been adopted by many organizations as a central part of their strategy to implement equal opportunities. It is interesting that attitudes towards different racial groups have been a continuing focus in scientific research into attitudes since at least the 1920s, both in terms of learning about attitudes *per se* and racist attitudes in particular. Even with that long history of research, the current debate on racism-awareness training centres on the same critical question. The basic premise of awareness-raising is that attitudes cause behaviour. To change discriminating behaviour to non-discriminatory behaviour therefore requires individuals to change their attitudes. Much recent research suggests that awareness-raising has not had this effect. One response to this by some organizations has been to abandon awareness-raising and to focus on making explicit what behaviour is required and what behaviour is proscribed, in for example job descriptions, procedural manuals and policy statements. This approach is supported by appropriate monitoring of behaviour and application of a disciplinary policy which details the penalties for non-compliance (see Wilson, 1996).

The two responses illustrate two different approaches to attitude change. I have described them to raise the critical question referred to earlier in this chapter – whether attitudes cause behaviour or whether behaviour causes attitudes. I believe that there is no dispute in the social sciences that there is a relationship between the two, and that it is generally accepted that there is a direct relationship. However, in which direction the arrow runs, ie which is cause and which is effect, is a question which remains unanswered with any finality. Some researchers argue that behaviour results from attitudes and others that attitudes result from behaviour. Awareness-raising assumes the former while the behaviour focus approach assumes the latter.

Some advocates of the behaviour approach may disagree with my last statement on the grounds that they discount attitudes as being irrelevant so long as behaviour conforms to what is required. My defence rests on two points. First, the existence of a relationship between attitudes and behaviour is demonstrated and therefore it is unrealistic to discount attitudes. Second, there are sound theoretical bases for focusing on behaviour as a means of changing attitudes and I would argue it is these that are being applied. In any case it is impossible to monitor all behaviour of all individuals all of the time in any organization and therefore the long-term effectiveness of the behaviour approach must rest on an assumption of changing attitudes.

Critical questions for practitioners

This discussion of the relationship between attitudes and behaviour raises a critical question for training and development practitioners: whether or not it is possible to change attitudes through training and development. The research referred to on racism awareness-raising suggests not. Other research, however, indicates a positive answer to the question. As the question of causal relationships is open it seems to me that answering the question rests on personal judgement. My own view will be given later.

There is a second important question which cannot be answered other than by personal judgement. Assuming training can change attitudes, or at least influence them, is it legitimate to do so? When asking what kinds of attitudes individuals hold the answer can only be in terms of positive or negative, desirable or undesirable, favourable or unfavourable, right or wrong. All of these labels imply value judgements. Changing attitudes therefore means judging some as 'right' and some as 'wrong' and then seeking to change the latter to conform to the former. But who determines what is the 'right' attitude? And from where is the legitimacy drawn to substantiate judging one attitude, 'right' and an alternative 'wrong'? These are obviously philosophical questions which can only be answered by individuals for themselves. In making that statement I betray to some extent my own personal philosophy which also encompasses the belief that all practitioners need to work through the questions for themselves.

Practical applications

Having briefly explored the scientific and philosophical aspects of attitude formation and change I will now turn my attention to more practical considerations. In my view attitudes certainly influence behaviour even if they are only one of the causes. For that reason they are important to the practice of training and development. Some of the key issues for individuals, organizations and training practice which arise from attitudes are:

- *Motivation*
  to perform, to learn, to change is influenced by individual attitudes.

- *Change*
  as we have seen is now the norm and attitudes which support flexibility and openness rather that rigidity are likely to be required for survival and growth.

- *Effectiveness*
  of individuals and organizations cannot be achieved if attitudes to work are outdated and irrelevant to changed conditions.

- *Detecting bias*
  is important since attitudes distort both giving and receiving information. Awareness of bias is essential for a degree of objectivity in information processing.

- *Learning*
  is made more difficult by the barriers created by negative attitudes to the content or the process.

Given the above list it is clear that training practitioners need to take account of attitudes and to seek to influence them. It is reasons such as these which in my view provide the legitimacy. It is both legitimate and possible for training activities to help individuals expose, examine and test the validity and utility of their attitudes towards learning and their topics of study. It is not possible in my view to change attitudes directly through training and development. Changing attitudes, and learning itself, is in the control of individuals. Training can, however, facilitate the posing and answering of questions of whether or not to change and in what direction. If that is the case then we need an understanding of what attitudes are, how they are formed and how they can be influenced.

THE NATURE OF ATTITUDES

Attitudes are difficult to define and no universally accepted definition is available. One which I find useful is:

An attitude is an individual's characteristic way of responding to an object or situation. It is based on the individual's experience and his or her interpretation of it and leads to certain behaviour or opinions.

There are three important points implicit in the definition which require further comment:

- Attitudes do not exist in the abstract. They only exist in relation to something concrete and specific. This may be an object or class of objects, eg, a particular person or group of people such as a manager or all managers, or a situation or class of situations, eg, delivering a particular lecture or delivering all lectures.
- Individual interpretation of experience is as important as the experience itself in explaining a particular attitude. For instance, two members of an audience who listen to the same 20-minute lecture apparently have the same experience. However, each person will interpret the experience differently and this different interpretation will in part explain any differences in attitudes towards the subject.
- Attitudes are a central part of what makes up an individual and unique personality. However, in common with other aspects of personality, attitudes cannot be directly observed. They can only be inferred from behaviour or expressed opinions. (In this context behaviour is direct action and verbal expression is excluded.)

Characteristics of attitudes

It is also clear that the definition tends to the view that attitudes are in part determinants of behaviour. This is consistent with my own view that attitudes are significant in influencing behaviour. Research into attitudes and their formation also suggests that attitudes:

- are always present though are mostly dormant. They become apparent through behaviour or speech in response to the object or situation;
- are reinforced by belief (cognitive domain); arouse strong feelings (affective domain); lead to behaviour (action tendency);
- consist of generalized and usually over-simplified favour or disfavour towards the object or situation;
- appear logical to the individual but often illogical and inconsistent to a neutral observer;
- are acquired through experience, ie learned, but often through subtle processes so that the individual does not recognize the attitude held or know how it was acquired. The process of socialization is significant here;
- can be rational or irrational. The intelligence of an individual does not mean rational attitudes;
- are rationalized and justified by the individual by (often unconsciously) selective illustrations and experiences;
- can be based on opinion or fact. Opinion-based attitudes may be more intense in expression and attachment;
- are often based on limited information/knowledge/experience;
- are learned, so they can be changed by the same process – by the individual.

Many of these characteristics are useful in informing attempts to influence attitude formation and change. For instance, the fact that an attitude and/ or the reasons for holding it may be unknown to the individual suggest that a useful starting point is often to make the attitude explicit. Because attitudes are usually over-simplified, illogical and based on limited information, simply exposing individuals to new information and/or experiences can sometimes be sufficient for them to adopt different attitudes.

METHODS OF ATTITUDE CHANGE

These two points are useful general guidelines in designing training activities which address the issue of attitude change. There are three broad categories of approach to attitude change, which are described in the next section.

Power/coercive approach

The first approach is referred to as the *power/coercive* model. The theoretical base is the behaviourist school of psychology and its application generally follows the principles of operant conditioning. In practice it involves the use of reward and punishment by those in authority to 'condition' the desired behaviour and so reinforce the associated attitude. The behaviour focus approach described earlier in relation to equal opportunities is an example of the power/coercive model in action.

In extreme form the model is also the basis of brain-washing techniques. At this level the approach can of course raise serious moral issues. However, a training technique which is based on similar principles has been developed. This is known as 'behaviour modelling' and is represented diagrammatically in Figure 10.4.

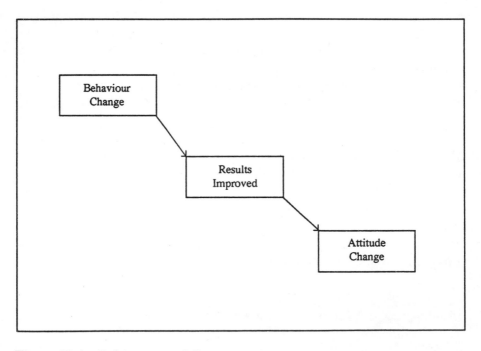

Figure 10.4 *Behaviour modelling*

Applying behaviour modelling in practice in simple terms consists of four related steps:

1. Produce specific, sequenced behavioural objectives for learning. These obviously apply to detailed descriptions of what the individuals will be required to do and say.
2. Provide a positive model of the desired behaviour. Written and verbal descriptions can work but visual stimulus is considered most effective. Learners must pay close attention to the model.
3. Allow repetitive and sustained practice of the desired behaviours.
4. Provide immediate and sustained feedback during practice. This has to be specific and behaviourally oriented. It should also contain both positive and negative feedback.

Some success has been reported for behaviour modelling but as far as I know it has not been widely adopted in its purest form.

The empirical/rational approach

A second approach to attitude change is known as the *empirical/rational* model. The theoretical base here is broadly cognitive psychology. The basis of the approach is to seek to persuade through logic and to appeal to rational self-interest. It is an approach which is widely applied in practice at what might be termed the 'macro' level. Examples of this are advertising campaigns, especially those conducted by government departments. A recent example is attempts to change attitudes towards sexual behaviour because of the risks from HIV. Elements of the approach are present in training activities though the only directly related technique I know of is in particular applications of the Repertory Grid.

The normative/re-educative approach

The third and final approach to attitude change is termed the *normative/re-educative* model (Bennis *et al*, 1976). This approach utilizes elements of the first two models but also applies theories from social psychology and sociology to do with social norms and peer group pressure. It is the basis of most attitude-focused training. In essence, the approach creates learning situations which encourage examination of existing attitudes and consider-ation of change. As with the empirical/rational model, responsibility for change or no change rests with and remains with the individual. There are three main stages in the approach – unfreezing, changing and re-freezing.

Unfreezing

Individuals will feel committed to their existing attitudes and the threat implicit in exposure and examination will also produce resistance. The aim of unfreezing is to overcome these resisting forces and create the motivation to change. There are three main steps in this stage.

1. Creation of a supportive and helpful atmosphere which is non-evaluative and non-judgemental.
2. Lack of confirmation. This means that individuals receive no support for expressed undesired attitude and related behaviour.
3. Disconformation. This means that individuals receive negative response/ reaction to expressions of undesired attitude and related behaviour.

Each of the above acts helps to unfreeze current attitudes and open the individual to learning new ones. This in turn leads to the next stage.

Changing

This stage provides potential alternative attitudes through the use of information and/or experiences which would have been rejected prior to unfreezing. Information is used to encourage adoption of new attitudes through two possible processes:

1. Identification. This involves the individual emulating attitudes and behaviour valued by significant others, eg, other members of the group or members of important reference groups. The Trainer, by definition, is also a 'significant' other.
2. Internalization. This involves facing and dealing with new situations and problems which support the adoption of desired attitudes. Training experiences designed to achieve this usually adopt the experiential learning cycle.

Re-freezing

The purpose of this stage is to 'freeze' newly adopted attitudes for long-term operation and impact. It requires continuing positive outcomes for the individual, otherwise newly adopted attitudes will themselves become discontinued. In organizational terms this normally implies the application of the power/coercive model through policies and procedures.

Conclusions

We can reach two conclusions from this discussion of attitude formation and change. First, that attitudes so far as is presently known are significant influences on individual behaviour and therefore must be on the agenda of bringing about individual change. Second, that it is probably legitimate and effective for training and development to make a contribution to such change through enabling individuals to:

- Identify and understand their current attitudes.
- Discuss with others the appropriateness and effects of current attitudes.
- Examine reasons for change and potential alternative attitudes.

SUMMARY

This chapter has examined the basis for theories of learning and attitude formation. It has described two theories of learning, both of which emphasize the engagement of the cognitive, affective and action domains in the learning process. Attitudes have been described as capable of change through learning and as of importance in bringing about change in individual behaviour. Any attempt to manage organization change must take account of attitudes and must utilize learning methods which reflect the principles common to System Beta and experiential learning.

There are a number of approaches to training and development which reflect these points and enable individual change through learning to be managed in ways which support organization change. As well as reflecting the theories described in this chapter, these methods also support the principles relating to organization change and changing groups described in earlier chapters. They therefore constitute important methods in training and development. Four such approaches are self development, action learning, structured group learning and self- and peer-assessment. All can be utilized as approaches to organization and team development as well as for changing individuals. An examination of the four methods forms the content of the next chapter.

support org. change = contributed to change within the org.

11. Approaches to individual change and development

A key message of this book is that managing change effectively requires the active involvement of those affected. This basic principle operates in all circumstances. The two types of circumstances we have been most concerned with are:

- Implementing a given change, eg, new operating procedures.
- Creating an organization more capable of managing change *per se*.

If active involvement is a basic principle then it must be applied to the contribution of training and development. This is particularly critical in the second application above since, as was argued in an earlier chapter, a learning organization requires learning individuals. In addition to or as part of involvement, managing change effectively also requires individuals who are capable of and willing to act independently and take responsibility for their own decisions. This again is particularly true in the second application. Managing change *per se* requires the encouragement of innovation and risk taking.

If these two points are valid then it must follow that traditional approaches to training and development which are based on models of direct instruction are inappropriate in the context of managing change. Such approaches can be valid for the maintenance needs of an organization. They are demonstrated as efficient and effective for the development of required knowledge and skills to carry out pre-determined tasks and to enable individuals to meet the performance requirements of well-defined jobs. However, they are less valuable where it is difficult to define performance requirements and where the nature of the job and the organization is dynamic. These features are, in this age of change, becoming true of more and more jobs and more and more organizations. (This does rather question the emphasis on and definition of competence being applied in national policies on vocational qualifications in the U.K.)

Traditional approaches have a further weakness in that the processes adopted have the effect of 'teaching' dependence. This means that individuals do not learn to think and act independently but rather learn to rely on others to provide direction. They also learn not to take responsibility as it is exercised for them by the Trainer.

What is required in the context of managing change are approaches to training and development which reflect the principle of involvement and which encourage the development of independence, innovation and responsibility. This chapter describes four such approaches. The first, self-development, in some ways reflects an overall philosophy rather than a specific methodology. The others apply the principles described so far and the philosophy of self-development in practical methods and techniques.

SELF-DEVELOPMENT

Self-development has been a growing approach to training and development in organizations for well over 20 years. The reasons for its growth are complex but probably reflect the following points:

- An increasing recognition of its value in managing change.
- Related to that, a recognition of the need to manage change.
- The unwillingness of many managers to accept traditional approaches to management development.
- A growth in supporting infrastructure, for example the availability of open and distance learning material and institutions providing these.

Defining self-development

It is difficult to define what exactly is meant by self-development since different writers take different views. My own definition is:

Individuals improving their knowledge, skills and abilities through their own self-directed efforts.

This definition does, I think, capture the essence of the approach. It will be clear from the definition that the approach reflects the principles of involvement and independence. It also implicitly includes the essential feature of learner autonomy which is inherent in creating independence and responsibility.

Some writers in their definitions of self-development distinguish between development *of* the self and development *by* the self. For them, each is a separate concept. The first refers to an individual deciding what is to be developed and how it can be achieved. After that point the actual development is carried out by another person, eg, a trainer if the individual attends a formal course or a manager if the individual requests a coaching session. The second concept applies only when individuals follow up the first set of decisions by carrying out the process of development themselves, eg, by reading a book or practising some skill. Personally, I find such a distinction leads to sterile debate and therefore my definition is intended to encompass either or both possibilities.

The process

Applying self-development requires the individual to consider and produce answers to three critical questions. The answers do not have to be definitive and in fact in most cases are likely to be tentative rather than certain. For most people this is beneficial, since flexibility is important. The questions are as follows:

'Where am I now?'
This requires some self-analysis to establish satisfaction or otherwise with current performance, usually linked to future requirements. The analysis should focus on identifying areas of strength and weakness in relation to both practice and ability.

'Where do I want to be?'
Answering this question should provide indications of what areas of performance will be worked on. It should also include the formulation of some learning objectives, target dates for completion, decisions on methods to be used and identification of resources available and required.

'How will I monitor progress?'
The individual needs to decide what measures will be appropriate to monitoring change and progress. A system and time-scale for regular review also needs to be developed.

It will be clear from this description of the process that my focus is job- and organization-oriented, although the same principles apply outside of those settings. Self-development will be most effective if individuals devote time and thought to managing their development activities. Planned and conscious development is likely to be more effective than ad hoc and unconscious development.

The questions examined
Probably the most difficult question is the first, especially in terms of self-analysis since it is often something new to most individuals. It is important to emphasize that self-analysis in this context does not normally imply the level associated with psycho-analysis and other clinical applications. The focus is intended to be work performance and job achievement. A focus on personal and career aspirations can also be included.

There is a useful two-stage process for posing and answering the first question. The first stage involves compiling a record of time spent on the various activities associated with doing the job. One method of classifying the results is as follows:

- *Where* the activity occurs, eg, own office, other office, external.
- *Who* else is involved, eg, boss, colleagues, subordinates, customers.
- *What* the activity is, eg, meeting, discussion, writing, thinking.
- *Size* or length of time it lasts, eg, 5 minutes, 5–30 minutes, 30–60 minutes.
- *Initiator* or who began the activity, eg, self, boss, subordinate.
- *Purpose*, eg, planning, deciding or monitoring.

It is important to have a classification system prepared before starting an analysis. Such an analysis is often a starting point in improving time management and there are many classification systems available commercially. The purpose in self-development though is to provide data for wider application. While the analysis will reveal the proportion of time being spent on different activities the identification of strengths and weaknesses as a basis for self-development requires a further stage of critical analysis. This is the second stage of the process which involves posing and answering questions such as the following:

- Why do I spend time on certain activities?
- Why do I avoid spending time on certain activities?
- What results am I achieving by the activities?
- Would different proportions of activities achieve better results?
- Which activities do I enjoy/not enjoy and why?

Answering questions such as these honestly can be very revealing of areas of need which can be tackled through self-development. Applying this two-stage process is therefore useful in answering both the first and second questions of the self-development process.

Some self-development methods

However, the two-stage process provides only a limited answer to the second question, ie, areas of performance to be worked on. The outcome is likely to be learning objectives. The analysis does not, however, determine what methods will be utilized to meet the objectives. In addition to formal methods such as courses and training programmes there are a variety of methods which individuals can utilize and manage themselves. Some of the most common are described in the following list:

- *Observation*
  An individual can begin to learn a lot simply by observing the behaviour of others. One example is in the area of interpersonal skills where observation of an effective negotiator can be very fruitful. Natural 'targets' for observation are the individual's manager, colleagues and subordinates.

- *Reflection*
  This refers to thinking about and analysing the results of observations. It is also includes reflection on the individual's own behaviour, performance and underlying reasons as a critical aspect of self-development.

- *Guided reading*
  Reading of text-books, journals and articles is an easy method of increasing knowledge. Seeking advice from those with technical or functional expertise will save time, money and effort. For example, if the analysis revealed a weakness in budgetary control then advice from an accountant on reading matter should be sought.

- *Visits/attachments*
  This is similar to guided reading though in this case time is actually spent with functional specialists. Spending a day or two or longer observing, talking to and perhaps working with staff in personnel, marketing or finance will increase both knowledge of those functions and understanding of their contribution. It will also increase ability in using techniques and systems, eg, cost control and human resource planning.

● *Seeking feedback*
This can be a slightly more risky method but feedback is essential in learning and development, especially in skill development. It is also important in terms of monitoring progress. Feedback is also rarely given if it is not requested. Natural 'targets' again include boss, colleagues and subordinates. The circle can be extended to friends and family especially where interpersonal skills are being developed. It is important, however, that self-developers choose their targets with care.

● *Seeking challenge*
If an activity is being avoided because of uncertainty over ability then effort can be made to engage in that activity more often to increase skill through practice. If supported by preparation through, for example, guided reading and by analysis of performance through, for example, feedback and reflection, this can be the most powerful method of self-development. Two simple instances of where the method would be appropriate are in giving presentations and in chairing meetings.

● *Prepared packages*
There is a whole range of self-study packages available on just about every subject imaginable. The media used range from print-based text to complex interactive-video programmes, now available for home use through interactive compact disc. These can be used to improve performance through learning and, where linked to qualifications, enhance career development. It is as well to remember that materials such as videos produced to support formal training courses can also be used by the self-developer outside of those contexts.

The list of methods is not exhaustive, nor should the methods be viewed as mutually exclusive. In practice a number of different methods will need to be used in combination in a self-development programme. Some of the methods can also be utilized in answering the third question in the process, ie, monitoring progress. For example, reflection and feedback are useful for that purpose and the end points of applying different methods, eg, a visit/attachment or a prepared package can provide logical time-scales for review.

It should be clear from the list of methods that the approach applies in practice the theories of learning discussed in the previous chapter. The principles of both System Beta and experiential learning are apparent in both the process and the methods of self-development. The use of processes such as Personal Development Plans is becoming more common, and provides one way of increasing the incidence of self-development as a step towards becoming a learning organization (see Chapter 6).

A note on open learning

The existence of wide-ranging prepared packages is one result of a growing interest in and use of open and distance learning methods in education and training. Part of the explanation for this growth lies in the application of new technologies for training purposes, such as computer based learning. In the UK at least another important factor has been government support based on a belief in the efficiency and effectiveness of such methods over more traditional education based methods.

My own view is that caution needs to be exercised (Stewart, 1987; Stewart and Winter, 1995). There is a distinction between open learning and distance learning. Distance learning simply means that the learner is not under the immediate and continuous supervision of a tutor or trainer. Learners do, however, rely on the services of a tutorial or training organization in planning the content, methods and media of learning. This in effect is the same as traditional methods based on models of direct instruction. The mode of delivery simply changes from face-to-face instruction to using text or visual images on paper or screens. By contrast, open learning implies flexibility of resource availability and autonomy for learners to choose the what and how of learning as well as the where and when. This definition of open learning reflects the same principles as self-development and the kind of approach required in managing change.

The problem is that imprecise definition and common usage has created a situation where many of the prepared packages are referred to as open learning, when in most cases they are in fact distance learning. Depending on how they are used they can reflect the principles of open learning, but this is often not the case, as the flexibility and autonomy inherent in open learning is missing and therefore distance learning packages do not necessarily form part of self-development or support a change orientation.

This is a complex argument which I hope I have simplified enough to demonstrate the key point. There are a range of other factors which affect the use of open and distance learning. Readers who are interested in pursuing the topic further are recommended to more specialist texts.

UTILIZING SELF-DEVELOPMENT IN ORGANIZATIONS

An organization peopled by self-developers is, in part at least, almost by definition a learning organization. It will certainly be one where continuous learning and development is a norm of behaviour and therefore part of the culture. This in turn will lead to increased flexibility and ability to cope with change: learning is an organization norm and therefore change is an organization norm. The abilities to anticipate, identify and respond to change are key components in managing change effectively, and these abilities are more likely to be present in an organization where self-development is adopted as an approach to training.

Introducing self-development

The question arises as to how self-development can be introduced as an organization approach. There are certain requirements for it to be possible. First, as in most features of organizations, the approach has to have the support and commitment of top management. Second, this commitment needs to be demonstrated. Two clear examples of how this can be achieved are in top management setting an example by engaging in self-development themselves and by incorporating their support in the organization's training policy. A third requirement also demonstrates the commitment. It is that realistic resources are allocated to support self-development. This does not imply that any individual can expect financial help with any development, nor that the only resource is money, although some companies such as Rover do 'put their money where their mouth is'! Time is just as important a resource as finance for self-development. Access to information and people is a similarly important resource which can be made available. A final requirement is in terms of management style. Soliciting feedback is unlikely to be popular in an autocratic organization. Questioning current performance and ways of working is similarly unlikely to happen in an organization where the emphasis is on doing things by the book. A style of management which encourages participation, questioning conventional wisdom, innovation and risk taking is more conducive to supporting self-development.

Training activities to support self-development

There are activities which can be undertaken by the training function which will encourage and enable self-development. These activities can also be useful in bringing about the required conditions. For example, they can be influential in development of a consistent and supportive management style. Some of the key contributions are discussed below.

Holistic management development
This simply means focusing on the whole person and enabling that person to manage the whole of their development. Out of this will come a recognition of the power of self-managed development. In turn this will lead to a supportive style being adopted by managers in relation to the self-development of their staff.

Self-development workshops
It may seem a contradiction but provision of off-job training events can be very useful in establishing self-development. The focus is usually on introducing the concept and process of self-development. Practice in applying the process can also form part of the activities. Participants can be made aware of the range and type of resources available, eg, people such as boss, colleagues, family and friends as well as physical resources such as books and packages, and the kinds of methods they can utilize. Such workshops can be included as part of management development and can also be made available more widely. I have experienced great success in running life and career development workshops for staff from administrative and clerical grades. Figure 11.1 provides an example of a framework I introduced to participants in the workshops. Self-development is not and should not be seen as the sole preserve of managers.

Learning-to-learn workshops
Developing the ability to learn is central to self-development. Formal workshops are again useful in introducing the concept of, for example, experiential learning. Work on identifying learning styles and improving weaknesses can also be included. This enables individuals to identify and maximize learning opportunities that arise in the course of everyday living and working. This in turn supports their practice of self-development. As with the previous items, such workshops can form part of management development programmes and can be made available more widely.

Resource centres
The training function can support self-development by providing easy and open access to resource centres. Materials included do not have to be sophisticated or expensive. It is nice to include prepared packages such as CBT or IV, but books, journals, articles and training resources such as videos can be equally valuable. A well-stocked and well-organized library is

Part One

1. List up to ten adjectives which describe you and your achievements with regard to:

    (a) *Your personal development and learning.*

    (b) *Your career to date.*

2. From the above lists, select the ten adjectives which describe you most accurately. Rank them in order 1 - 10

    1.

    2.

    3.

    4.

    5.

    6.

    7.

    8.

    9.

    10.

3. Re-group the above adjectives into the following categories:

    Positive   *Neutral*   *Negative*

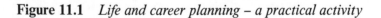

Figure 11.1   *Life and career planning – a practical activity*

4. Now write a short statement summarizing areas of satisfaction and dissatisfaction in relation to career development, and strengths and weaknesses in relation to personal development.

    Career Development:

    Personal Development and Learning:

Part Two

You have so far been establishing where you are today and the experience of the past. This section is about where you would like to be in the future.

5. List below 5 goals you would like to achieve in the future in relation to career development. Be imaginative but realistic, creative but specific. Think in terms of 3 to 5 years.

    Career Goals

    1.

    2.

    3.

    4.

    5.

6. Now do the same for personal development, eg things you would like to learn or do.

    Personal Development Goals

    1.

    2.

    3.

    4.

    5.

Figure 11.1 *Life and career planning – a practical activity* (contd)

7. Now rate the priority of each of your goals according to the following scale.

   HP - Compared to other goals, this is very important.
   MP - This goal is moderately important.
   LP - Compared to other goals, this is unimportant.

8. Now rate the ease of achievement of each of your goals using the following scale.

   HA - Compared with other goals, I can easily achieve this one.
   MA - This goal will be moderately difficult to achieve.
   LA - Very difficult to achieve.

9. Select from the list of goals above those which are currently most important to you. Confine your list to 5 priority goals. Rank them in order of importance.

   1.

   2.

   3.

   4.

   5.

10. Now write a short statement making a promise to yourself that you will achieve ONE of the goals within six months.

Figure 11.1 *Life and career planning – a practical activity* (contd)

an effective resource. Study facilities such as desk and chair in a quiet room are also important resources.

Self-development support groups
As a concept support groups are important in training and development activities in managing change. The other approaches described later in this chapter build them in as a critical feature. Self-development is essentially an individual activity, but it can be supported by regular contact with others engaged in similar activity. Trainers can facilitate the establishment and operation of self-development support groups. Allowing the time for meetings of such groups is one example of allocation of resource by top management. The training function can act as a clearing house of names to put people in touch with one another and can provide a Process Consultancy service to groups to help them to function effectively.

Acting as 'honest broker'
A final activity is to act as a link between different parts of the organization. For instance, it may be that individuals want to arrange short visits or attachments to departments outside their own, or perhaps to other organizations. The training function can help in arranging and facilitating such activities simply by maintaining a list of contacts and putting people in touch with each other. Alternatively, someone may need advice on guided reading. Again, the training function can provide a link between the self-developer and the functional expert.

Conclusion

Self-development as an approach to individual development has a lot to offer organizations wishing to improve effectiveness in managing change. It is an approach which also offers a real opportunity for training specialists to make an effective contribution. It does, however, have a potential weakness – the fact that it is relatively unstructured. While this may be an advantage from the point of view of the individual it may be a drawback for the organization if individual learning does not transfer into organizational learning. One approach which reflects the principles of self-development but overcomes the weakness of relating and sharing in terms of the organization is action learning. This is described in the next section.

ACTION LEARNING

Action learning is an often misused term. It does not mean simply learning by doing. Rather, it is a very specific approach to and method of management development devised by Revans (1976; 1980; 1982). The key feature of action learning mirrors self-development in that it requires managers to take responsibility for their own learning, and in so doing develops the ability to manage, to learn and to manage learning.

Reg Revans, as the inventor, chief proponent and most experienced practitioner of action learning, emphasizes the near futility of writing and talking about action learning. This futility is best explained by the assumptions inherent in the term 'action learning' which implies a process of learning from action. Revans' theory of learning explained in the previous chapter reinforces the point. However, Revans usually emphasized the futility of writing and talking *by* writing and talking about action learning and so I will accept his permission to write about it here. I hope I do the method justice since my own experience of participating in and managing action learning programmes supports Revans' point on futility but has also convinced me of the effectiveness of the method.

Underlying assumptions

Action learning contains a number of underlying assumptions related to managing and learning; each set of assumptions is discussed below.

Managing

- Managing occurs in conditions of ignorance, confusion and uncertainty.
- Managing is about the discovery of appropriate solutions to pressing problems in those conditions through the posing of effective questions.
- The search for effective questions and the choice of solution involve personal risk on the part of managers and reveal, whether recognized or not, their personal values.

Learning

- Learning involves the re-ordering and re-structuring of existing knowledge, not the acquisition of new knowledge.
- There is a distinction between knowing in the sense of being *able to*, and knowing *about* something. The former is the purpose and result of learning – not the latter.
- Learning follows action and does not, as the dominant theory of learning in education implies, precede it.

Discussion of assumptions

It is perhaps worth commenting on these assumptions. I have yet to meet a manager who, being honest, would disagree with the first set. This is especially the case with the first one. Although it was true when action learning was first formulated in the 1950s it is, in the conditions being faced by organizations today, more critical for it to be recognized and more difficult for it to be denied. The third assumption about management is equally important. The role of managerial values has long been recognized, not only by Revans but also by OD practitioners such as Blake and Mouton (Blake and Mouton, 1978). There is now a resurgence of focus on values as the critical component of organization culture and ultimate survival (Brown, 1995).

The assumptions on learning are more open to challenge, not least because they are in part a consequence of and reaction to Revans' own experience of being a practitioner in management education. They are, in my view, valid. Revans gives an interesting example of the operation of the first. The fact that apples fell to earth was known well before the birth of Isaac Newton. The workings of the solar system were similarly well known to others. It was re-ordering and re-structuring existing knowledge which enabled Newton to discover the law of gravity and formulate the consequent theories. The second assumption is I think self-explanatory. We can only be confident learning has occurred when learners can do something they could not do before. The third assumption is supported by System Beta and experiential learning. It is expressed in the way it is to challenge the conventional wisdom which underpins the formal system of education predominant in Western society. This conventional wisdom is for me best illustrated by a character in a television play written by the British dramatist David Leland. The play is entitled *Flying Into The Wind* and the character, a school inspector, utters the line, 'As long as Laura is not in school she is not learning anything, is she?' That line neatly captures the beliefs about learning and related attitudes towards education and training which Revans seeks to challenge through action learning.

The nature of action learning

Following on from these assumptions, Revans believes that managers learn best with and through each other by tackling real problems in real time. Action learning is designed to organize management development so that these beliefs can be put into practice. It involves the following:

- *Projects*
  Participating managers learn through undertaking a major project which tackles a real problem being experienced by a real organization.

- *Expertise*
  Subject-matter experts, for example in finance, marketing or personnel, are available to provide inputs on theory and technique as and when the managers decide it will be beneficial. It is entirely possible for their services not to be requested.

- *Sets*
  Participants are formed into small groups of between four and eight members. These groups are referred to as 'action learning sets'. Each group meets separately on a regular basis to critically review progress of the individual members. The set is also a support group and critical vehicle of development.

- *Set adviser*
  Each set in an action learning programme has the help of a set adviser. The role of the adviser is to facilitate the operation of the group and it is not concerned with teaching. Advisers are usually experienced in action learning and can often be past participants. The role demands skills similar to those of a Process Consultant.

These features of action learning programmes have a number of important consequences. Those which are most critical in understanding the nature of action learning are:

- *Syllabus*
  The syllabus of action learning programmes is under the control of participating managers. They, rather than trainers or academics, decide what they wish or need to learn. The same is true to an extent of the methods used to learn. Outside the overall design of a programme, those decisions also belong to participants.

- *Self as content*
  Because of the challenge of a real project and unfamiliarity with the problem being tackled, participants learn much about themselves. This learning is extended and shared through the operation of the sets. Thus, managers engaged in action learning programmes learn about themselves

as individuals and, to use Revans' phrase, as 'a cohort of comrades in adversity'.

- *Nature of management*
  Again as a consequence of projects and sets, participants learn the real nature of their responsibilities and tasks as managers. They also learn about the nature of organizations.

- *Organization learning*
  Organizations involved in action learning programmes derive real benefit. They learn how to learn by posing effective questions. This in itself illustrates the value of the approach in managing change.

This description of action learning is necessarily brief and leaves a lot unsaid. It should be clear, however, that the approach reflects the principles discussed at the beginning of the chapter. Participants are fully involved, independent and focus on relevant, personally owned needs. They are also through the processes involved learning to manage change in themselves and in organizations.

Applications of action learning

Action learning was originally devised as an approach to management development, and that has been its major application to date. There is, in my view however, no reason in principle why similar designs cannot be used for other purposes and contexts. Professional development, administrative and clerical staff, technical grades and operative-level training can all benefit from action learning. The point of utilizing the approach at operator level is in fact demonstrated: the use of Quality Circles is now well established for operators. The use of this approach to managing improvement and responding to changes in the operating environment has been widely adopted in the USA, UK and Europe. The Japanese 'inventors' of Quality Circles have acknowledged their debt to Revans in explaining that the idea is based on the principles of action learning.

There are, however, some practical problems in operating pure action learning outside of management development. This follows from Revans' descriptions of problems and projects.

Problems and projects
We have seen that Revans distinguishes problems from puzzles. Action learning projects should ideally be concerned with problems and not

puzzles. The need to make decisions and live with the consequences is an essential feature of action learning. It can be difficult to identify or even create suitable projects which reflect this requirement for staff who are not managers. This difficulty is not insurmountable of course, but it does exist.

As well as being focused on problems, projects should also have two phases – diagnosing and applying. Participants in action learning programmes should not only investigate a problem, they should also be required to work for implementation of their solutions and learn from the consequences. This again can be difficult to organize for non-managerial staff. It has also been identified as one of the problems in operating Quality Circles for production staff (Legge, 1995).

A final difficulty arises from the settings of projects. There are four possibilities:

- Own job – participants focus on a problem in their own job.
- Different job/own organization – here participants tackle a problem in a different department, eg, an engineer examines a marketing problem.
- Own job/different organization – in this case there is an exchange of staff between organizations participating in a programme, but individuals tackle problems related to their own specialism, eg, a personnel manager from a hospital completes a project to do with recruitment and retention in a manufacturing company.
- Different job/different organization – here too there is an exchange of staff between organizations, but individuals move out of their functional specialism for their projects, eg, a production manager from manufacturing tackles a marketing problem in retail.

The benefits are greater in the last two settings, for both the individual and the organization. The original programmes set up by Revans had only those two possibilities as essential design features. More recent programmes have adopted the first two settings as compromises in the absence of a sufficient number of participating organizations. They do have the advantage of being easier to organize. Programmes for non-managerial staff are more likely to be limited to the first or second setting, and purists could legitimately argue that in that case it is not really action learning, although Revans himself has endorsed all four settings as potentially effective.

The third approach to individual change and development I want to examine does not share these difficulties. It can be applied to any type of job and staff from all levels. It can also be used as an approach to organization development and for team development purposes.

SELF- AND PEER-ASSESSMENT (SAPA)

The term 'self- and peer-assessment' is something of a misnomer on two counts. First, the process is more concerned with development than it is with assessment. It is in practice a development method rather than a means of educational assessment. Second, to the extent that it does involve assessment, it is self-assessment as opposed to peer-assessment. The role and function of peers is to aid the process of self-assessment.

The process was originally devised by John Heron, the founder and first Director of the Human Potential Research Project at the University of Surrey (Stewart, 1986). The initial application and development of the method was with education and health service professionals in the UK. It has now been applied internationally and in all sectors of economies. The purpose and process of SAPA is summarized in Figures 11.2 and 11.3.

Underlying assumptions

As with other approaches, SAPA rests on a number of assumptions which are worth making explicit:

- Assessment of self and others is a natural human process which is capable of being managed and used productively.
- There is very little, if any, true objectivity in assessment of work performance and therefore assessment is strengthened if its subjective nature is recognized.
- Performance criteria generated by those doing the job will be more relevant and realistic.
- Individuals and groups will be more committed to standards and goals set by themselves rather than those imposed from outside.

The last two assumptions are central to the thrust of this book and so do not require further comment. The first is normally accepted by most people without major difficulty. It is the second which usually causes problems. Acceptance depends on personal judgement which in turn is dependent on individual values. My rationale in favour of acceptance rests on the view that management is not an exact science and therefore apparently objective measures such as X sales per month or Y widgets produced per week are chosen as a subjective decision. Whether sales or widgets matter very much is dependent on personal values in relation to a particular economic system. Assigning specific numbers to X and Y certainly involves subjective

<u>Purpose</u>

The purpose of self and peer assessment is to help individuals to identify their performance, strengths and weaknesses in doing their job and to work out and implement action plans that will remedy weaknesses.

<u>Process</u>

Assessment takes place with a group of peers. The process is voluntary in that each person chooses to be a member of the group and chooses how far they want to go with their own personal assessment.

The process is as follows:

1. The group identifies an area of performance that it collectively wants to address.

2. The group defines the criteria of master performance within this area, so as to provide yardsticks by which members can assess their performance.

3. Members of the group choose criteria from the list which they personally want to assess themselves against. (It is possible and reasonable that each member will choose different criteria).

4. Each member of the group (if they choose to) assesses themselves against chosen criteria. This is done privately and forms the self assessment part of the process.

5. Peer assessment starts with an individual sharing his/her self assessment with the group in order to get feedback. The type of feedback is chosen by the individual from a range of possibilities.

6. The individual may then re-appraise his/her assessment and shares the re-appraisal with the group.

7. The individual may then construct an action plan with or without the help of the group. If the group is used they are asked to make suggestions for possible action to overcome weaknesses.

    Each individual in the group goes through stages 5, 6 and 7 in turn. The assessment reaches an end when the last member completes stage 7.

8. The group reviews the session and then decides when next to meet.

Figure 11.2 *Self- and peer-assessment*

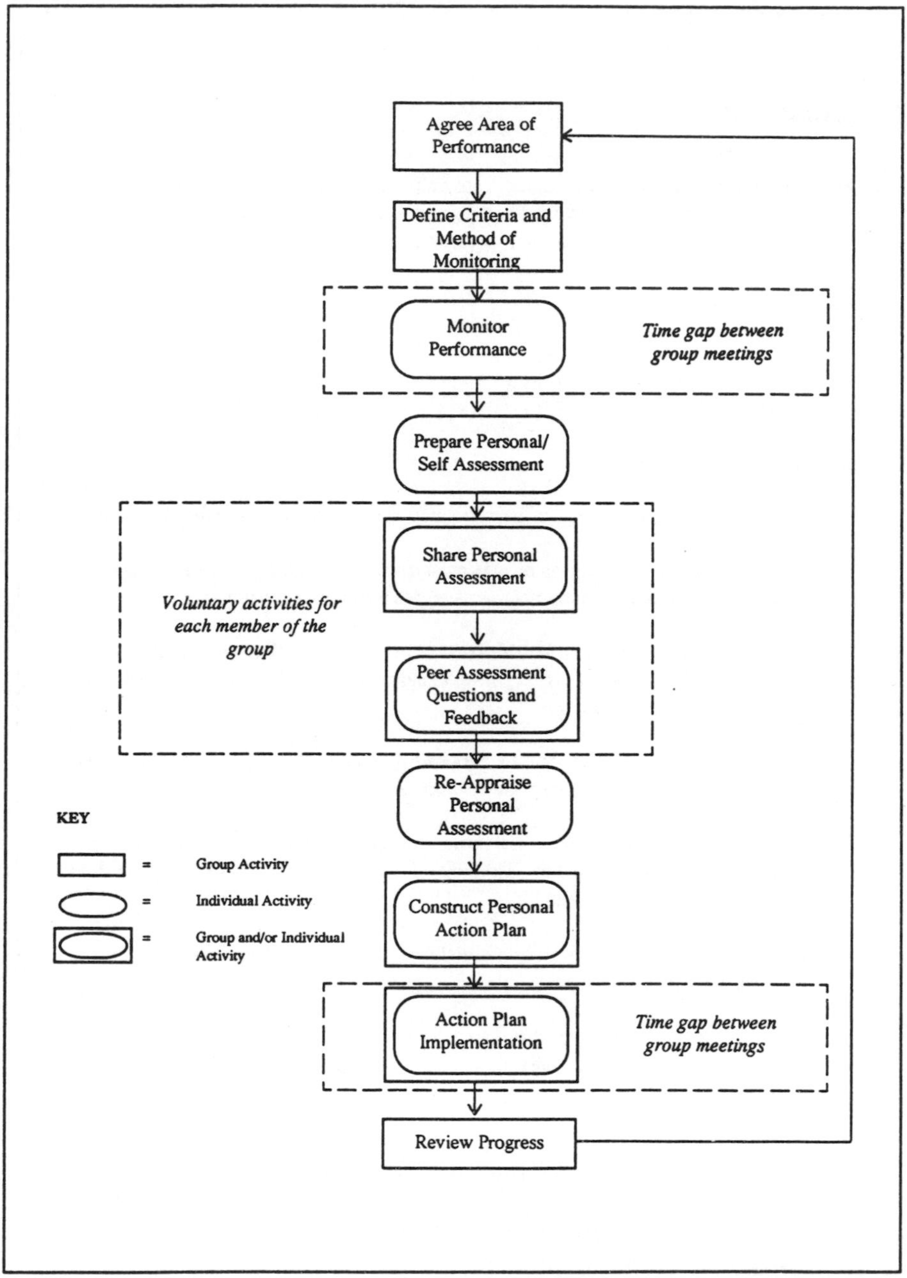

Figure 11.3 *Self- and peer-assessment – stages in the process*

judgement since the future cannot be known and it is that which setting standards of performance is seeking to manage.

The process in practice

There are a number of points which need to be explained about parts of the process and using it in action:

- Engaging in the process and any stage within it needs to be voluntary. It cannot be imposed.
- Stages 1 and 2 in Figure 11.2 usually adopt the brain-storming technique as a means of generating data. Essentially these stages consist of agreeing the following:

  Area of performance   –   What are we looking at?
  Criteria of performance   –   What are we looking for?
  Standard of performance   –   How much should we have?

- There are certain choices and rules attached to feedback in stage 5:

  - it can be limited to questioning;
  - questions can be either clarifying or challenging;
  - questions should focus only on the personal assessment;
  - feedback can include both positive and negative comments;
  - positive alone can be chosen;
  - if negative is chosen positive must also be chosen and given last;
  - feedback must be owned by the person giving it and its subjective nature recognized in the words used. Feedback statements therefore should be prefixed with words such as 'I think', 'I feel', 'In my experience of you', etc;
  - feedback can range outside of the personal assessment but must focus on the agreed area of performance and criteria.

- There will normally be an agreed time period, usually four to six weeks, in an operating SAPA group between Stages 3 and 4. This allows for personal monitoring of performance, usually through a method devised and agreed by the group.
- Group members are responsible for managing the process in the time available. Most operating SAPA groups meet for roughly half a day every four to six weeks.

- As an egalitarian process the time allocated for Stages 4 to 6 is usually divided equally between group members. Each member then decides how they want their allotted time used in terms of sharing their personal assessment and their chosen types of feedback.
- Review of progress and decisions on moving into new areas of performance are usually standard items of business at group meetings.

Introducing SAPA into organizations

My own experience of SAPA now extends to tutoring approximately twenty one- or two-day workshops for trainers or potential participants; facilitating four operating groups in three different organizations for varying lengths of time; being a participating member of two groups in two different organizations; and using the process as an approach to team development with three separate teams from three different organizations. Based on that experience I have reached a number of personal conclusions:

- Trainers should experience the process before using it with others.
- Trainers should participate in the process with the groups they facilitate.
- Most new groups require the services of a facilitator for an average of six meetings.
- Open workshops can be a useful way of introducing the process into work organizations.
- Working with natural groupings of staff, ie, those doing the same or similar work, is most effective.
- Management support is desirable though not essential. It is, however, essential if the purpose is organization, as opposed to individual or team, development.
- The process is itself developmental in skills such as time management, creativity, questioning and feedback. It also builds confidence and motivation.
- Utilizing SAPA is likely to identify weaknesses in the organization as well as individuals, eg, ineffective systems or inappropriate policies.
- SAPA groups provide a support system which is with individuals outside of formal meetings.
- Both of the preceding points can be threatening to managers.
- SAPA can provide a vehicle for identifying and meeting training needs.

My experience has also demonstrated that SAPA is a powerful development tool for organizations, teams and individuals who wish to use it. It can and does improve current performance significantly. More importantly in this context, it develops skills and attitudes supportive of coping with change. It involves and gives responsibility to organization members. As with self-development, SAPA also helps to build a culture of continuous learning and change. In addition, participants develop an outward and future-oriented approach to their work and development. This is essential in managing change, not least in guarding against complacency and insularity.

STRUCTURED GROUP LEARNING (SGL)

Perhaps the greatest strength of the three approaches discussed thus far is also their greatest weakness. It is their change orientation which means they are inappropriate when dealing with the maintenance needs of organizations. The final approach we will examine *can* be utilized in that context and for that purpose. In common with the other approaches, SGL fosters independence and responsibility through involvement and control. It also utilizes the dynamics of groups to shape attitudes and, almost as a by-product, develops the skills of effective team working.

Origins and rationale of SGL

SGL is a derivative of an approach termed 'Instrumented Team Learning' which was developed by Blake and Mouton for use in their Grid OD programmes (Blake, 1978; Mouton, 1984). It is soundly grounded in experiential learning as a theoretical base and has its roots in the group-based methods utilized in 'T' Group training by NTL in America and the Tavistock Institute in the UK. The rationale for SGL can be summarized as follows:

- Structure provides constructive and helpful direction to learning.
- The learning designs of SGL provide the support of access to 'expert' materials but leave responsibility with the learners.
- The learning designs require and therefore ensure full involvement of all group members.
- Because of the absence of a trainer within the group, participants have to manage time, direct their own learning, resolve differences, etc. These responsibilities help build group effectiveness and teamwork skills.
- Each design utilizes a 'Review of Group Effectiveness' to help this process.
- Learning is in part a social process and effective groups produce effective learning.

These assumptions have I hope by now been well established in this book. The meaning and operation of those which are perhaps less clear will become more apparent as SGL is further explained.

The SGL procedure

As already indicated SGL is an approach which seeks to apply the experiential learning cycle. It does this by following a common procedure on formal training programmes. A starting point is to form the total participant group into small groups or syndicates of between four and seven members. These small groups will work together throughout the programme. The procedure then consists of the following four stages being applied to each learning objective:

1. Individual activity.
   Individuals, working alone, complete a given task, eg, read a text, complete a questionnaire, produce a sample of work.
2. Syndicate activity.
   Working in their sub-groups, individuals are directed to reach group agreement on the individual task or share the results.
3. Intergroup activity.
   Syndicates combine in the total participant group to assess their work, sometimes by using a scoring mechanism or by comparison with other syndicates.
4. Syndicate review.
   Individually and collectively in their syndicates participants review both the *content* of their work, eg, have we met the learning objectives, and the *process*, eg, how well did we work together, what do we need to do to improve.

It will be clear that as well as the experiential learning cycle this procedure also seeks to apply the theories of groups discussed in Chapter 7. It also attempts to overcome the potential weaknesses of experiential learning when applied in formal training programmes, especially in terms of inefficiency or ineffectiveness in knowledge acquisition.

SGL designs

SGL is based on a set of basic designs. These are considered to be capable of dealing with any knowledge or skill-related learning objective. The three most commonly used designs are summarized in Figure 11.4.

Title	Method	Application
1. Shared Group Learning Design	Individuals study material and then complete self-test. Syndicate groups then complete self-test and compare results against model answers.	Knowledge Acquisition
2. Shared Group Teaching Design	Individuals study part of total material. Then they 'teach' other members of their syndicate group. Individual completion of self-test.	Knowledge Acquisition
3. Performance Judgement Design	Group generates criteria to judge performance. Individuals then perform task and assess against agreed criteria, followed by further practise if necessary.	Skill Development

Figure 11.4 *Three SGL designs*

It is interesting to note the similarities between SAPA and the Performance Judgement Design. The similarity is illustrative of the common principles which run through all of the approaches described in this chapter. Such principles are also indicative of the common thread which runs throughout the book, that is, that involvement, responsibility and independence on the part of individuals are the key to managing organization change.

There is a fourth SGL design which is concerned with attitude formation and change. It also follows these principles and, in common with the designs in Figure 11.4, is applied by using the SGL procedure described earlier. An example of what is called Attitude Clarification Design is given in Figure 11.5. This is an activity which I designed for use on programmes addressing the issues of equal opportunities in employment.

EXAMINING AND CLARIFYING ATTITUDES

ON EQUAL OPPORTUNITIES - STEP ONE

A variety of attitudes can be held by individuals toward the issue of equal opportunities. In the space provided, you are asked to write a brief description of what your present attitude is toward each of the items listed. Your answer should picture how you presently feel about the topic. Please spend a maximum of 15 minutes on this activity.

1.   Equal opportunity means ....

2.   Individuals and groups affected by lack of equal opportunities include ....

3.   Equal opportunities is important as an issue because ....

4.   Organization policies on equal opportunities should ....

5.   Equal opportunities in practice as well as policy can be achieved by ....

6.   The contribution of training to equal opportunities is ....

7.   The role of individuals in achieving equal opportunities is ....

EXAMINING AND CLARIFYING ATTITUDES

ON EQUAL OPPORTUNITIES - STEP TWO

Using the individual responses as a source of information, each group is asked to reach agreement on what they consider to be the soundest answer to each item.

It is suggested that for each item one member begins the discussion by explaining their answer to other group members so that they understand how the individual feels about the issue. Then another member explains their answer, and so on. This revealing of personal attitudes forms the basis for arriving at a group agreed answer.

It will be helpful to individuals for each group member to keep a personal record of the group's conclusions. The group should be ready to report their results in a maximum of 60 minutes.

Figure 11.5   *Attitude Clarification Design – an example*

Using SGL in practice

It should be apparent that use of SGL as intended in the original design of the method has certain implications for trainers. There are basically two roles to be adopted and each can be performed by the same or different individuals:

1. Preparing SGL designs and instruments, perhaps in conjunction with subject-matter experts. The latter are likely to be required for knowledge applications related to technical or professional subjects.
2. Managing and processing the actual training event where the designs are applied.

Processing the last two activities in the SGL procedure perhaps calls for the greatest skill on the part of the trainer. It is important to understand that SGL designs and instructions for their use are usually paper-based and the trainer simply hands them out. Instructions also contain time targets and the trainer is required to enforce these. These procedures add certain pressures to group working with which the trainer has to be able to deal. Using SGL on formal training programmes creates a different type of relationship between the trainer and the participant group. Most trainers find the relationship threatening and difficult to deal with at first. However, my own experience of using SGL for many purposes with many groups confirms that it is a useful and worthwhile approach. Another word of caution is worth recording: producing effective materials is not an easy task and the method is preparation-intensive.

Conclusion

We can summarize the basic philosophy and operation of SGL as follows:

- *Structured*
  Using trainer-designed instruments, participants are helped to meet their learning objectives through structured experiences.
- *Group*
  Participants work in small groups to provide cooperation and competition, with increasing effectiveness at working together being both a major purpose of, and vehicle for, learning.
- *Learning*
  Acquisition of appropriate and required knowledge, skills and attitudes.

Seen in that light, many trainers will recognize that they do in fact apply the principles and variants of SGL if not the precise method. The strength and value of the principles lies in applying and fostering involvement, responsibility and independence. Doing so in relation to the maintenance needs of organizations and in the context of traditional, formal training programmes has the effect of encouraging individuals to adopt positive attitudes towards learning and change. Training and development can therefore make a positive contribution to the effective management of change in all of its activities.

SUMMARY

This chapter has described four approaches to individual change and development which are supportive of creating a learning organization. Such an organization will be peopled by individuals committed to and capable of managing their own development. Self-development helps to create that condition. Such an organization will also utilize approaches and mechanisms which encourage and facilitate mutual learning, and the dissemination and sharing of individual learning. Action learning and SAPA help to create that condition. Such an organization will not forget to pay attention to its maintenance needs but will also seek to foster involvement, responsibility, independence and innovation in meeting them. SGL and similar approaches help to create that condition.

The approaches described in this chapter are not, therefore, mutually exclusive. They can all be used in any combination for different but mutually supportive purposes, which all help to create a learning organization which is, by definition, more effective at managing change.

The approaches also almost bring this book to an end. They perhaps most clearly and easily demonstrate the kind of contribution training and development can make to managing change. There are, however, two further models that I have developed which help to inform both managing change, and the contribution of training and development. They are described in the final chapter.

12. The role and contribution of training and development

This book has examined a wide range of theories and models relevant to managing change in work organizations. These in turn have been shown to underpin a range of approaches, methods and techniques which can be utilized by training practitioners. I would argue that applying these in practice will enable the function of training and development to remain relevant to organizations by making a real contribution to the effective management of change. This argument rests in part on the proposition that change is now the norm and is likely to represent the single biggest challenge in the 1990s and beyond.

The purpose of this final chapter is to attempt to bring together the major threads contained in the book. This is not an easy task since the book includes a diverse and complex set of ideas at the three levels of organization, group and individual. There are, however, some key principles which emerge and which apply both to managing change *per se* and to training and development contributions. I intend to show what those principles are by introducing two final models which represent the results of my own thinking. One is an overall framework of managing change. The second is designed to aid decisions on training and development activities. I will also provide some ideas on an overview of the role and contribution of training and development in managing change. The chapter and therefore the book will close with an alternative view of the whole subject of managing change. This will hopefully have the effect, if by now you are convinced by my arguments, of causing you to think again!

AN OVERALL FRAMEWORK OF MANAGING CHANGE

It seems to me that the evidence of everyday experience fails to support a notion that individuals naturally or by definition resist change. All of us embrace many changes in our lives. Some of these are fairly minor and of relatively little consequence, eg, a new hairstyle, a mode of dress, or a new car. Others such as moving house, getting married or changing job or career are more important and are pursued with perhaps more thought. Once a decision to change is taken, it usually generates a high degree of commitment and enthusiasm. Yet other changes are even more significant in a person's life and involve a re-appraisal of beliefs and values, for example getting divorced, changing religion or switching political allegiance. Even these fundamental changes are not resisted just for the sake of it though equally they are not likely to be embraced lightly.

Essential conditions

There are, I believe, two conditions inherent in all these changes experienced by individuals which determine and create lack of resistance and produce commitment. The first is that they are in the control of the individual; they result as a consequence of a personal decision. The second is that individuals expect beneficial outcomes; that is, they believe embracing the change will make their lives better, happier, or more satisfying. The lesson seems to be that change will be embraced by individuals in organizations if those conditions are present.

An amusing way of representing one of these conditions is contained in the following formula:

Change happens when A B + C D > E F and G H

where

A B = Alternative Benefits;
C D = Current Dissatisfaction;
> Is greater than;
E F = Energy Forecast;
G H = General Hassle.

What is being said is that change will be embraced if it is perceived as being likely to bring about an improvement which is worth the cost of achieving it. The expression of the condition in the formula is based on the expectancy theory of motivation and so it has academic credentials. What it also implies is that the decision to change or not is a personal one and therefore there is implicit support for the first condition – individual control, as well as the second – beneficial outcomes.

Applying the conditions to organizations

Applying this argument to organization change, it seems to me that there are only four reasons why individual members do not embrace change:

1. They do not have the ability.
2. They do not know of the change.
3. They do not believe the change.
4. They do not agree with the change.

The first is obviously a straightforward training and development issue, which will be examined in more detail in the next section. The second is a too-common reason in organizations. Often top and senior management make decisions and adopt policies or strategies that require individuals to behave differently. These are either not communicated at all or done so ineffectively, with the result that staff continue to behave in the established way and fail to adopt new behaviours simply because they are unaware of a requirement to change. The third reason is also not uncommon. Communication in terms of transmitting the information is effective but staff do not believe that the organization really desires the change. The feeling is that managers are not really serious and are simply 'going through the motions' or 'paying lip-service' to some new fashionable concept or legal requirement.

Some examples of these two reasons operating in practice may be helpful. I was once asked to provide some management training for junior managers in an organization that was subject to increasing competition and was performing ineffectively in response. Prior to the changed market situation the organization had enjoyed relatively easy success and therefore had adopted a fairly lax approach to cost control. There was a need now for a much more cost-conscious approach to the work and effective operation of cost-control procedures. Perhaps I was naïve but I was amazed to discover that the junior managers did not know of the market conditions or the organization's poor performance. The planned training became something of an irrelevance once that situation was rectified.

Many organizations have experienced failure in trying to implement concepts such as Team Briefing or Total Quality Management (TQM). The same is even more true of taking on legislative requirements such as Health and Safety procedures or, to take a UK example, the Data Protection Act. In these cases members of staff are required to behave differently, ie, they have to change the way they do their jobs. The fact that they do not is often explained by a disbelief in the organization's commitment to the change. While they know of the change individuals do not believe that they are really required to adopt it by the organization. It is in overcoming this reason that the old adage 'actions speak louder than words' is never more true. Organizational members take their cues from what top and senior managers actually do rather than what they say.

The fourth reason simply reflects the two conditions described earlier. In order for individuals to adopt a change and be committed to it they have to feel some control over the decision to change and be convinced of some beneficial outcomes. The first of these conditions is not necessarily true in all cases if the second is clearly present. This is particularly the case if the change does not impact on personal beliefs and attitudes. Generally, change is more likely to be adopted if individuals are *involved* in decision making.

The nature of this involvement can vary depending on the nature of the change. If it is of minor significance, for example similar in personal terms to changing one's hairstyle, then the involvement can remain at an intellectual level. If it is of major significance, for example similar in personal terms to changing one's religion, then the involvement has to include examination of beliefs and values. Involvement also has the benefit of dealing with the other reasons for non-adoption of change. If individuals are involved they will know of the change and believe managers are serious about it as well as being more likely to agree with it. The whole of this argument is represented in the model given in Figure 12.1. It demonstrates both that involvement is necessary and that the nature of involvement will vary according to the nature of the change.

USING TRAINING INTERVENTIONS

Essentially, individual behaviour change requires two conditions to be met:

1. Learning has to occur.
2. Motivation to apply the learning has to exist.

What I have argued so far in this chapter in terms of involvement is intended to ensure the second condition is met. Meeting the first condition is an obvious role for and contribution of training and development. It also addresses the first reason why individuals do not embrace change, ie, lack of ability.

We have seen in previous chapters that the nature of training interven-

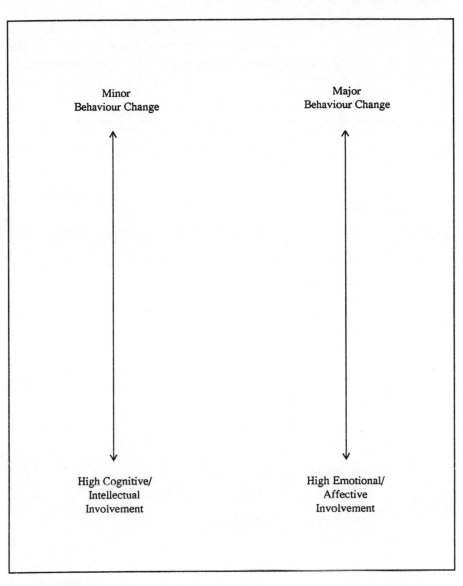

Figure 12.1 *A framework for managing change*

tions has to reflect the principle of involvement and have the effect of building personal responsibility, independence and innovation. From the framework in Figure 12.1 however, it is clear that the sort of involvement

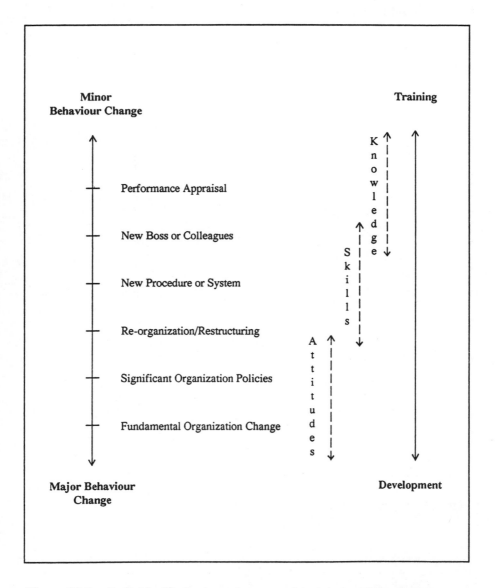

Figure 12.2   *Individual behaviour change and training and development*

will vary according to the nature of a particular change. Training interventions also have to reflect this principle.

The focus of training and development

The focus of training in individual terms is development of knowledge, skills and attitudes. The balance of emphasis between these three characteristics is likely to reflect the nature of the change being managed. In general and broad terms those changes which can be classified as minor are likely to require knowledge-based learning while those that are classified major are likely to require learning which focuses on attitudes. This argument forms the basis of my second model in this chapter, shown in Figure 12.2. It focuses on the relationship between training and development and individual behaviour change.

The model explained

Some words of explanation will help understanding and use of the model. An important general point needs to be made first. The model focuses on individual behaviour change because that has been, and to a large extent remains, the traditional focus of training and development. It is also a continuing and legitimate focus for training interventions designed to help manage change. However, the model applies equally well to teams and whole organizations. Bringing about and managing change at those levels also involve learning in relation to knowledge, skills and attitudes and requires differences in emphasis according to the nature of the change. The following paragraphs provide the additional explanatory points.

Training and development
The distinction between training and development is meant to illustrate the difference between formal/traditional training activities and those concerned with personal development. Traditional activities which adopt didactic methods are likely to be most relevant at the 'minor' end of the change continuum. Conversely, those methods such as SAPA, described in the previous chapter, which focus on personal development are likely to be most effective with 'major' changes.

Minor versus major changes
The change continuum from minor to major is a little difficult to apply in practice, because the definition of what is minor or major lies in the perception of those affected. A given change or set of requirements, eg, those arising from adopting TQM, may be perceived and experienced as major by

some and as minor by others. As a general rule though, it is likely that behaviour associated with individual beliefs, values and attitudes will constitute a major change.

Some examples may help to illustrate the operation of the continuum:

- *Performance appraisal*
  This may require only a slight and therefore minor change in behaviour. The individual simply requires the knowledge of what is required, eg, a 10 per cent increase in performance targets.

- *New boss or colleagues*
  This usually means that individuals need to behave in slightly different ways but again only need to know in what ways.

- *New procedure or system*
  This moves down the continuum. Individuals will be required to adopt new ways of behaving which require extensive new knowledge and some skill development.

- *Reorganization/Restructuring*
  This is now getting closer to a major behaviour change. Individuals are likely to have changed roles and responsibilities which certainly implies new knowledge and skills and possibly attitudes.

- *Significant organization policies*
  Here we are in a situation which requires significant changes in behaviour which to a large extent are influenced by personal values and attitudes. Thus a major change is implied. Adoption of equal opportunities employment policies is one example.

- *Fundamental organization change*
  Examples include those organizations which move from the public sector to the private sector or from a production orientation to a market- and customer-led philosophy. Such change can imply a new paradigm of work for individuals affected and therefore it is classified as major. The recent and current experience of the UK financial services industry, particularly banking, is one example where this may apply.

It will be clear that these examples move through the continuum from minor to major. They also help to illustrate the distinction and application of training versus development activities. Some development-focused training interventions would include examples such as British Airways' 'Putting People First' programme or Rover's 'Working With Pride' initiative.

Knowledge, skills and attitudes
The final explanatory point is simply to recognize that all HRD interventions involve all three characteristics of knowledge, skills and attitudes. I have argued earlier in the book that the most simple training activity will have an impact on individual attitudes to the organization, the job and future learning. The model, however, is meant to suggest difference in *emphasis* rather than content or processes. Knowledge needs to be emphasized at the minor end, skill in the middle range and attitudes at the major end. Based on my experience, this is a valid and useful guide to decisions on methods and approaches to adopt.

Figure 12.2 is the final model I want to present. It does I believe reflect many of the theories and models in the book and, together with Figure 12.1 represents a useful synthesis of my key arguments. There are however two further sets of ideas which I want to offer which reinforce the main arguments. The first is a discussion of the overall contribution of training and development to managing change. The second identifies some of the implications for training practitioners.

THE OVERALL CONTRIBUTION OF TRAINING AND DEVELOPMENT

The training function has a number of contributions to make to the management of change. The first, and perhaps most critical, is to ensure that the 'people' issues and implications of change are raised and understood by organizational decision makers. Failure to do this is often a reason why planned change does not work or why organizations respond too late or ineffectively to environmental change.

A second contribution lies in helping individuals, especially managers, develop their ability to cope with change itself. Personal development programmes and team development activities can be designed to build the coping skills required to live easily with the ambiguity and uncertainty which invariably accompany change. I find it useful to do this by focusing on the life experiences of individuals and encouraging them to examine personal changes such as those identified earlier, eg, getting married and becoming a parent. Such programmes can also encourage risk taking by allowing for experiment in a supportive climate. Being able to take risks in situations of uncertainty is useful, if not essential, in coping with and managing change.

Management development provides opportunities for a third contribution. Programmes can have those items identified in the last paragraph as a major theme. They should always, in my view, enable managers to fulfil their responsibilities for developing their own staff. As Salaman (1995) argues, managing is in essence concerned with managing learning. Managing the learning process as it occurs in doing work is, in any ase, an essential component of a learning organization. This requires managers who are effective developers of people. Training can also help managers in this through appropriate support mechanisms and materials.

The fourth contribution can also form part of management development but has wider application. It is simply providing knowledge and skills in utilizing change processes. Appropriate training can develop in managers at all levels the knowledge and skill required to gain commitment to change – an essential ingredient in managing change. Trainers can also provide direct consultancy and advisory services on applying change processes in particular contexts. As part of this, provision of training activities can make a contribution to overcoming the three barriers of knowing, believing and agreeing.

The fourth barrier of ability leads to a fifth and perhaps most obvious contribution. It is often the case that a specific change will create a need for new knowledge and skills to be available within the organization and to enable individuals to continue to perform effectively. Training and development contributes here through diagnosing training needs and implementing appropriate strategies to meet them. The management of change can never be complete or effective unless arrangements exist to develop the necessary ability to meet the consequences of a given change.

There is a sixth and equally important contribution. It is a proper and useful function of training and development to encourage and enable individuals, groups and the organization to both regularly review their current performance and to raise their heads above the parapet to survey the operating environment. Trainers are well placed to facilitate open discussion on performance, to contribute expertise in helping to diagnose causes of poor performance and to help identify where and how improvements are possible. Unless such activities take place regularly, downward trends in performance may only be identified when it is too difficult to reverse them. Internal change in response to the environment can only be managed effectively if external change is identified early enough and responses planned in advance. Trainers have a key part to play in developing an outward-looking and future-oriented approach to managing the organization. Such an approach requires that time is devoted to examining and analysing significant features of the operating environment. Examples of training interventions that can help this process include strategy workshops and team development programmes for senior managers.

These six contributions represent a summary of what is possible. No doubt they can be added to. The contents of this book will hopefully enable practitioners to offer those contributions I have identified. They do, however, suggest some critical implications for practitioners, implications which are supported by some of my own research and that of other writers.

IMPLICATIONS FOR TRAINING PRACTITIONERS

My research into the changing role of MD practitioners identified a number of characteristics which will be expected of them in the future by employing organizations (Stewart, 1990b). These expected characteristics will also be required if practitioners are to perform the activities associated with the overall contribution of training and development to the management of change. The key items are:

- An ability to think strategically.
- Possession of a clear vision of the future of the organization and the contribution of training and development to creating that future.
- An ability to promote and market training and development towards areas of strategic need.
- Having the energy and enthusiasm for training and the organization.
- An ability to work with and through others in varying roles and functions within and outside the organization.
- Being a competent manager.

These requirements can be said to be essential for a further two reasons. One is that practitioners will be required to act as agents of change within organizations. The focus of this work will be primarily the attitudes of managers towards organization change. A second is that practitioners will need to operate easily and effectively at all levels of the organization. This means being equally comfortable dealing with top managers examining strategic direction and with junior managers and their staff working on operational problems. At whatever level they are working, practitioners have to ensure relevance of their services to the mainstream business of the organization and live operational problems.

Practitioner values

There is one further characteristic that needs to be mentioned. It is in my view the most important and is likely to determine the success or otherwise of attempts to contribute to managing change. It is the issue of practitioner values.

Edgar Schein (1988) has identified the major challenge facing organizations as that of achieving external adaptation and internal integration. This refers to effective management of external and internal sources of change. What strategies and responses are adopted to meet this challenge is a matter for organization decision makers. It is not the job of training practitioners. This means that the practitioner has to adopt a neutral stance.

Of course, as professionals, practitioners should provide advice and will have an important input to those decisions. Personal values will dictate a personal position. However, once decisions are made, the practitioner must adopt a position of having no opinion on whether strategies are right or wrong, good or bad. The role at that point is to provide professional services to aid implementation.

Neutrality, then, is the first practitioner value. It also brings additional advantages. It is likely to lead to avoidance of the negative effects of organizational politics. Alignment with one faction or another will not help in demonstrating the required characteristics or putting them into practice. Neutrality is also likely to be helpful in building trust in the practitioner throughout the whole organization. This is essential in working with and through others.

There are two further necessary values. The first is to be problem-oriented. Managers and organizations tend to look for and adopt quick-fix solutions, often at the expense of a complete and thorough problem analysis, which leads to inefficiency and ineffectiveness. Training practitioners provide a useful service by focusing the attention of everyone on the problem. The final value is related to and follows from this. It is to be non-prescriptive. Practitioners should avoid offering 'ready-made' solutions. They should also avoid taking over responsibility from those who own the problem by providing their own prescriptions. Being non-prescriptive will ensure practitioners remain problem-oriented and that they are not making decisions which rightfully belong to others.

AN ALTERNATIVE VIEW ON MANAGING CHANGE

In this final section I wish to acknowledge an alternative view. The book as a whole has supported a view of involving those affected in managing change. It has done so in the belief that this will bring efficiency and effectiveness in organization functioning. There is, of course, a counter argument which suggests the opposite is true. Involvement is time-consuming and results in compromise which fails to address the problem, and is therefore both inefficient and ineffective. One example of this view is what I call the 'Thatcher approach' to managing change.

The 'Thatcher approach' to managing change

I have named the approach 'Thatcher' since it characterizes what I judge to be the basis of managing change adopted by governments led by Mrs Thatcher as Prime Minister in the UK between 1979 and 1990. Those governments created and implemented significant change in all aspects of British life. They did so largely without following traditional processes of consultation and negotiation through Green Papers and White Papers. This is not to say that White Papers in particular have not been issued. It is however the case that the time periods for responses have been much shorter than previously and that responses which were negative to proposals have been largely ignored.

The basis of managing change in the Thatcher approach has been to use the legislative and executive power available to push changes through, and to ignore the protests, complaints and resistance tactics of those who disagree. Society as a whole and individual members have simply been required to like it or lump it, and accept the consequences of the latter option.

The other critical aspect of the approach is to do with ignoring the 'howls of protest'. It seems to me that this rests on the assumptions implicit in the following questions:

- In two years who cares?
- In five years who remembers?

I pick the time-scales simply to illustrate the point. Given time, people will cease to resist and therefore accept change, and given more time the change will in fact become the norm. It will no longer be different and people will have difficulty recalling what the pre-change situation was really like.

Such an approach is available to organizations. Indeed it has been and is commonly used by work organizations. The Thatcher approach is not the exclusive preserve of governments whether in the UK or elsewhere.

Organizations have legislative and executive powers too and the administrative mechanisms for implementation. The combination of massive redundancies in order to 'rightsize' together with culture change programmes experienced in, for example, the UK banking sector, illustrates attempts to apply both approaches.

SUMMARY

Determining which approach is more efficient and effective – the one inherent in the arguments in this book or the Thatcher approach – is a matter of judgement. The question cannot be answered with certainty. The judgement is only partly intellectual. At that level I must admit to some minor doubts though they are not serious. In the final analysis the judgement is, I think, a matter of personal values. In those terms I have no doubts. The basic principle of involvement, together with its application to produce independence, responsibility and innovation is the most efficient and effective approach to managing change. Certainly, I think, applying both at once creates contradictions which, in the end, are irreconcilable.

The preceding sentences sit well with my personal values. They 'feel' right. In my experience the same is true of most training practitioners. If it is true of you I hope you find this book of continuing help in putting your values into practice for the benefit of the organizations for which you work and the individuals who inhabit them.

Bibliography

Anthony, P. (1994) *Managing Culture*, Open University Press, Buckingham.

Ardrey, R. (1967) *African Genesis*, Collins, London.

Ardrey, R. (1970) *The Social Contract*, Collins, London.

Ardrey, R. (1977) *Territorial Imperative*, Fontana, London.

Argyle, M. (1989) *The Social Psychology of Work*, 2nd edn, Penguin, Harmondsworth.

Argyris, C. (1970) *Intervention Theory and Method*, Addison-Wesley, London.

Argyris, C. and Schon, D.A. (1978) *Organizational Learning: A Theory in Action Perspective*, Addison Wesley, London.

Bandura, A. (1977) *Social Learning Theory*, Prentice-Hall, London.

Bateson, G. (1972) *Steps to an Ecology of Mind*, Ballantine, New York.

Belbin, R.M. (1981) *Management Teams: Why they Succeed or Fail*, Heinemann, London.

Bennis, W.G. (1969) *Organisation Development, Its Nature, Origins and Prospects*, Addison-Wesley, London.

Bennis, W.G. *et al* (1976) *The Planning of Change*, 3rd edn, Holt Reinhart and Winston, London.

Blake, R.R. and McCanse, A.A. (1991) *Leadership Dilemmas: Grid Solutions*, Gulf Publishing Co, Houston.

Blake, R.R. and Mouton, J.S. (1978) *The New Managerial Grid*, 2nd edn, Gulf Publishing Co, Houston.

Blake, R.R. and Mouton, J.S. (1985) *The Managerial Grid III: The Key to Leadership Excellence*, 3rd edn, Gulf Publishing Co, Houston.

Brown, A. (1995) *Organizational Culture*, Pitman Publishing, London.

Buckley, R. and Caple, T. (1995) *The Theory and Practice of Training*, 3rd edn, Kogan Page, London.

Burgouyne, J. *et al* (1978) *Self Development Theory and Applications for Practitioners*, Association of Teachers of Management, London.

Burns, T. (1966) *The Munugement of Innovation*, Tavistock, London.

Campbell, T. and Cairns, H. (1994) 'Developing and Measuring the Learning Organization: From Buzz Words to Behaviour' in *Industrial and Commercial Training* **26**, 7.

Dawkins, R. (1989) *The Selfish Gene*, 2nd edn, OUP, Oxford.

De Bono, E. (1982) *Lateral Thinking for Management: A Handbook*, Penguin, Harmondsworth.

Fisher, C. (1996) 'Managerial Stances: Perspectives in Manager Development' in *HRD: Perspectives, Strategies and Practice*, Stewart and McGoldrick.

Francis, D. and Woodcock, M. (1990) *Unblocking Organisational Values*, Scott Foresman and Company, London.

Fredericks, J. and Stewart, J. (1996) 'The Strategy-HRD Connection' in *HRD: Perspectives, Strategies and Practice*, Stewart and McGoldrick.

French, W.L. (1984) *Organisation Development*, 3rd edn, Prentice-Hall, London.

French, W.L. and Bell, C.H. (1990) *Organization Development*, 4th edn, Prentice Hall, Hemel Hempstead.

Garratt, R. (1988) *The Learning Organisation and the Need for Directors Who Think*, Gower Publishing, Aldershot.

Garvin, D.A. (1993) 'Building a Learning Organization' in *Harvard Business Review*, July/August.

Handy, C.B. (1985) *Understanding Organisations*, 3rd edn, Penguin, Harmondsworth.

Handy, C.B. (1990) *The Age of Unreason*, Arrow Books, London.

Hinings, R. (1983) *Planning, Organising and Managing Change*, Local Government Training Board, Luton.

Honey, P. and Mumford, A. (1986) *The Manual of Learning Styles*, Peter Honey, Maidenhead.

Honey, P. (1988) *Face to Face*, 2nd edn, Gower Publishing, Aldershot.

Honey, P. and Mumford, A. (1989) *The Manual of Learning Opportunities*, Peter Honey, Maidenhead.

Huczynski, A. (1987) *Encyclopaedia of Organisation Change Methods*, Gower Publishing, Aldershot.

Hunt, J.W. (1986) *Managing People at Work*, 2nd edn, McGraw-Hill, Maidenhead.

Jahoda, M. (Ed) (1973) *Attitudes: Selected Readings*, 2nd edn, Penguin, Harmondsworth.

Jashpara, A. (1993) 'The Competitive Learning Organization' in *Management Decision*, **13**, 8.

Johnston, R. (1996) 'Power and Influence and the HRD Function in *HRD: Perspectives, Strategies and Practice*, Stewart and McGoldrick.

Kolb, D. *et al* (1984) *Organisational Psychology*, 4th edn, Prentice-Hall, London.

Lee, R.A. (1985) *Organisational Behaviour*, Hutchinson, London.

Legge, K. (1995) *Human Resource Management: Rhetorics and Realities*, Macmillan Press, Basingstoke.

Lupton, T. (1983) *Management and the Social Sciences*, 3rd edn, Penguin, Harmondsworth.

McGoldrick, J. and Stewart, J. (1996) 'The HRM-HRD Nexus' in *HRD: Perspectives, Strategies and Practice*, Stewart and McGoldrick.

Margulies, N. (1971) *Organisational Development: Values, Process and Technology*, McGraw-Hill, New York.

Mayon-White, W. (Ed) (1986) *Planning and Managing Change*, Harper & Row, London.

Moorby, E. (1991) *How to Succeed in Employee Development* McGraw Hill, Maidenhead.

Moss-Jones, J. (1994) *Learning Organization: Concepts, Practices and Relevance*, NHSTD, Bristol.

Mouton, J.S. (1984) *Synergogy: A New Strategy for Education, Training and Development*, Jossey-Bass, London.

Mumford, A. (1980) *Making Experience Pay: Management Success Through Effective Learning*, McGraw-Hill, Maidenhead.

O'Shaughnessy, J. (1976) *Patterns of Business Organisations*, Allen & Unwin, London.

Pedler, M. *et al* (1986) *A Manager's Guide to Self Development*, 2nd edn, McGraw-Hill, Maidenhead.

Pedler, M. *et al* (1991) *The Learning Company: A Strategy for Sustainable Development*, McGraw Hill, Maidenhead.

Peters, T.J. and Waterman, R.H. (1982) *In Search of Excellence*, Harper & Row, London.

Pfeiffer, J.W. (Ed) (1973–89) *The Annual Handbook for Group Facilitators*, University Associates, California.

Pfeiffer, J.W. (Ed) (1985) *A Handbook of Structured Experiences for Human Relations Training*, Vols 1–10, University Associates, California.

Racism Awareness Training: A Critique (1987), London Strategic Policy Unit, London.

Revans, R.W. (1976) *Action Learning in Hospitals, Diagnosis and Therapy*, McGraw-Hill, Maidenhead.

Revans, R.W. (1980) *Action Learning*, Blond and Briggs, London.

Revans, R.W. (1982) *Origins and Growth of Action Learning*, Chartwell & Bratt, Bromley.

Ribeaux, P. and Poppleton, S.P. (1978) *Psychology and Work*, Macmillan, Basingstoke.

Salaman, G. (1995) *Managing*, Open University Press, Buckingham.

Schein, E. (1969) *Process Consultation*, Addison-Wesley, London.

Schein, E. (1988) *Organisational Psychology*, 3rd edn, Prentice-Hall, London.

Senge, P. *et al* (1994) *The Fifth Discipline Fieldbook*, Nicholas Brealy Publishing, London.

Senge, P.M. (1990) *The Fifth Discipline: The Art and Practice of the Learning Organization*, Doubleday, London.

Stewart, J. (1986) 'Self and Peer Assessment: A Development Tool', *Training and Management Development Methods*, **1**, 1.

Stewart, J. (1987) 'Open and Distance Learning – The Required Revolution', *Journal of ITD*.

Stewart, J. (1989a) 'Effective Team Skills – A Diagnostic Model', *Training and Management Development Methods*, **3**.

Stewart, J. (1989b) 'Bringing About Organisation Change – A Framework', *Journal of European Industrial Training*, **13**, 6.

Stewart, J. (1990a) 'The Contribution of Training to the Management of Change', *Journal of ITD*.

Stewart, J. (1990b) *The Contribution of Management Development to the Local Government of the 1990s*, Local Government Management Board, Luton.

Stewart, J. (1994a) *Organization Development: History, Perspectives and Relevance to NHS Organizations*, NHSTD, Bristol.

Stewart, J. (1994b) 'The Psychology of Decision Making' in *Decision Making: An Integrated Approach*, D. Jennings and S. Wattam (Eds), Pitman Publishing, London.

Stewart, J. and McGoldrick, J. (Eds) (1996) *HRD: Perspectives, Strategies and Practice*, Pitman Publishing, London.

Stewart, J. and Sambrook, S. (1995) 'Practitioner Views on HRM and Environmental Change', unpublished working paper, Nottingham Business School.

Stewart, J. and Winter, R. (1995) 'Open and Distance Learning' in *The Handbook of Training and Development*, S. Truelove (Ed), Blackwell Publishers, Oxford.

Stewart, V. (1990) *The David Solution: How to Reclaim Power and Liberate Your Organisation*, Gower Publishing, Aldershot.

Stoner, J.A.F. (1989) *Management*, 4th edn, Prentice-Hall, London.

Toffler, A. (1971) *Future Shock*, Pan Books, Basingstoke.

Tushman, M. and Romanelli, E. (1985) 'Organization Evolution: A Metamorphosis Model' in *Research in Organization Behaviour*, **7**.

Tyson, S. and Jackson, T. (1992) *The Essence of Organizational Behaviour*, Prentice Hall, Hemel Hempstead.

Watson, T.J. (1994) *In Search of Management*, Routledge, London.

Williams, A. (1989) *Changing Culture*, IPM, London.

Wilson, D.C. (1990) *Managing Organisations*, McGraw-Hill, Maidenhead.

Wilson, D.C. (1992) *A Strategy of Change*, Routledge, London.

Wilson, E. (1996) 'Managing Diversity and HRD' in *HRD: Perspectives, Strategies and Practice*, Stewart and McGoldrick.

Woodcock, M. and Francis, D. (1979) *Unblocking Your Organisation: A Practical Guide to Organisational Change*, University Associates, California.

Woodcock, M. and Francis, D. (1981) *Organisation Development Through Team Building*, Gower Publishing, Aldershot.

Index